HEALTH
and
FAITH

MEDICAL, PSYCHOLOGICAL
AND RELIGIOUS DIMENSIONS

Edited by
John T. Chirban

UNIVERSITY
PRESS OF
AMERICA

Lanham • New York • London

Copyright © 1991 by

University Press of America®, Inc.

4720 Boston Way
Lanham, Maryland 20706

3 Henrietta Street
London WC2E 8LU England

Library of Congress Cataloging-in-Publication Data

Health and faith : medical, psychological, and religious
dimensions / edited by John T. Chirban.
p.   cm.
Includes bibliographical references and index.
1. Holistic medicine.   2. Medicine and psychology.
3. Medicine-Religious aspects.   I. Chirban, John T.
R733.H39   1991   610—dc20   91-13342 CIP

ISBN 0–8191–8284–2 (cloth : alk. paper)
ISBN 0–8191–8285–0 (paper : alk. paper)

 The paper used in this publication meets the minimum requirements of
American National Standard for Information Sciences—Permanence
of Paper for Printed Library Materials, ANSI Z39.48–1984.

Health and Faith: Medical, Psychological and Religious Dimensions

Table of Contents

Introduction

The papers presented in this volume offer interdisciplinary sensitivity to critical matters of health from the perspectives of medicine, psychology, and religion. By drawing upon expertise of leaders in these fields, this collection of papers provides a holistic understanding of illness and cure. The papers of this volume are selected from interdisciplinary conferences which argue for the return to approaching human health holistically, while maintaining the strengths of the independent dimensions of inquiry. This interdependent perspective emphasizes the integrity of the disciplines and affirms their joint interest.

Part One, "Healing: Science and Faith," introduces how these three disciplines can work in an interdependent way toward their distinctive as well as their shared goals. In my article, "Healing and Spirituality," I discuss the spirit of the Christian tradition concerning health and its relationship to modern healing disciplines. Rev. Dr. Demetrios Constantelos explains the relationship between faith and the scientific disciplines in the course of church history and through its antecedents in the Greek religion and suggests how models of faith and science in history serve as prototypes for today. Bishop Nicholas provides a theological perspective for critical ethical decisions in his discussion of particular technological advances.

Part Two, "Genetic Engineering: Where Do We Draw the Line," discusses the impact of medical technology for modern life. Dr. Peter Diamandis identifies the potential problems of scientific advances and the need for sound ethical decision making to shape the future of human life. Rev. Dr. John Breck offers guidelines for addressing such concerns and recommends the organization of an interdisciplinary committee to assist in this interfacing of science and religion.

Introduction

In Part Three, "Depression: A Case Study," three professionals from the disciplines of medicine, psychology, and religion present the case of a man suffering from clinical depression, each drawing upon the resources of his particular discipline. Dr. John Demakis provides a medical perspective; Dr. Nicholas Kokonis, a psychological perspective; and Rev. Nicholas Krommydas, a theological perspective.

Part Four, "AIDS and Cancer: The Role of the Helping Professionals," offers articles that deal with the most crucial health problems of modern times. Dr. George Pazin considers the medical, psychological, and theological implications of AIDS in his article "HIV and AIDS: Impact on Life in the Twenty-first Century." Chaplain Peter Poulos then discusses direct care of AIDS patients for professionals and laymen alike, and Rev. Dr. Milton Efthimiou clarifies the roles of values, ethics, and direct service in "AIDS: Is it a Moral Crisis?" Following this presentation is a special committee report by experts in the helping professions, who convened to address questions about AIDS and the religious community. Georgia Photopulos then shares her experiences in her battle with metastic cancer and discusses how the helping disciplines and faith may offer help for the patient.

In Part Five, "Miracles and Technology," Dr. Theoharis C. Theoharides explains a scientific approach to miracles and scientific discovery, and Rev. Dr. John Meyendorff works to interrelate the perspectives of the disciplines concerning this topic in his article, "Miracles: Medical, Psychological, and Religious Reflections." Rev. Constantine Sarantidis, in his article, "God, Miracles, and Quantum Mechanics," compares and relates how miracles can be understood in modern times. Finally, Karen Piligian takes into consideration the interdisciplinary contributions of medicine, psychology, and religion in her discussion of how *touch* serves as a vehicle for miracles as it heals people.

John Chirban

Boston, Massachusetts

Part One

Healing: Science and Faith

Healing and Spirituality

John T. Chirban

Healing has been a subject of fundamental interest for humans and has attracted the finest talent within civilization since the time of recorded history. The topic of healing provides a natural link for various disciplines in society through such fields as medicine, psychology, and religion. It is a subject that has tremendous spiritual implications because healing unifies a person and thereby brings him or her toward wholeness—holiness.

I. HEALING

The work of Jesus Christ is to a great extent an account of healing: restoring, curing, making whole. In part, the personal activity of assisting in the healing of others helps to align our lives with Christ. Participating in this healing process gives our lives meaning. It is through the face-to-face encounter of healing through sacraments, prayer, miracle, or love that we witness the power of God's life force, which nurtures body, mind, and soul.

Healing may well be the single greatest challenge that we can have. But how are we to heal others? And how do our approaches to healing relate to what is being done by professionals and non-professional alike?

Our culture seems to have an acute preoccupation with and interest in healing. The approaches used to achieve healing are quite diverse. People want to be better

3

in body, mind, and soul and often use extraordinary approaches to achieve this end. For example, some Olympic athletes not only exercise to achieve excellence but inject steroids as well. Before studying, some students check their biorhythms, consult their horoscopes, or take vitamins. Some seek to experience heightened states of spirituality outside of the usual religious norms. One Jewish woman, whom I have seen in private practice, left Reformed Judaism and now uses astro-projection and crystals to meet her friends on planets other than earth: these women believe that they meet on other planets to share their friendship even though they live hundreds of miles apart.

From the perspective of the formal disciplines of medicine, psychology, and religion, healing is considered a valued goal because it consists of the rightness, wholeness, and soundness of body, mind, and soul. But even though these fields share a common goal—healing—they have rarely shared mutual understanding and appreciation with reference to their methods towards these goals.

Approaches to healing and, most unfortunately, those individuals served by the various approaches to healing, are recipients neither of the Hebraic nor the holistic view of man—the latter being an approach valued by the Church Fathers— but rather the results of the classical Greek ideas of dualism and rationalism in the care of body, mind, and soul.

Ever since Hippocrates—especially in the last five centuries—a division has taken place that relegates the care of man's physical well-being to the medical pro-fession and the care of man's spiritual being to the Church realm. The denial of the supernatural origin of disease seems to have accelerated the progress of the medical sciences and created the subsequent high esteem in which they are held today. While medicine has increasingly gained in importance—to the point of possessing a monopoly on the authority to heal—the physical being—the Church's philosophy of healing the whole person has decreased in importance and its healing role has been limited to the spiritual dimension. To a large extent, modern-day disciplines, such as medicine, psychology, and religion, germinated during the period of the scholastics. A tension was created between the approach of these disciplines to healing and the Patristic approach, which is existential, holistic, and concrete.

Clearly, this fragmented approach to understanding humanity and addressing its needs has resulted in valuable contributions from these disciplines. However, this climate has left "healers" isolated and parochial—at one extreme feeling overly confident of the healing powers they have derived from their corners of investiga-tion, which they might perceive as the fullness of life, to the other extreme of being fearful that their perceptions may be invalidated by the professional criteria of other disciplines.

In reality, the strict following of only one method of healing is rarely compre-hensive and is hardly ever practiced by lay people today. Few Christians are con-verts to the notion that they should become devotees of only one approach to healing. Nonetheless, some have a dilemma of whom to call when not feeling well: a priest for prayer or exorcism; a psychologist for an antidepressant or psychotherapy; or a physician to identify the physical cause for an ailment.

Because of this fragmented approach to health, people are seldom clear about how to be healed or, for that matter, what constitutes good health. The offer of a potpourri of approaches and choices leads one to ask, "Does anyone really understand my pain and my needs?"

Furthermore, inconsistencies and ambiguities often exist in what is said and what is done in the area of health. For example, one may be told to have faith in order to be healthy yet when not feeling well be treated with scientific intervention, being unclear about how such decisions are made. What health care and spiritual providers are saying and what they are doing seem in such instances to be at odds.

In the face of a pluralistic society that seems to affirm all things and usually commits itself to none, we must not be surprised but rather empathize with the individual who experiences this lack of direction and ultimate disharmony of body, mind and soul. It should be no surprise that individuals often do not have confidence in the standard methods of these disciplines and feel left to orchestrate their own plans to meet their physical, psychological, and spiritual needs.

There is, however, another side to our modern plight. Although healing seems to have been interpreted by closed scholastic systems, a renaissance for the appreciation of the whole person is currently in progress. Attempts are being made to transcend the method of compartmentalizing man into body, mind, and soul and to describe a multidimensional unity in which each of these areas is considered to have influence on the other dimensions.

A. In the Field of Medicine

Medical schools are now establishing departments of behavioral medicine (in effect, incorporating the healing methods of psychology) and physicians are leading research on the value of meditation (in effect, incorporating the healing methods of religion) in treating both the causes and cures of physical ailments. For some time we have known how emotions affect physical health, such as how stress creates ulcers or even cancer, but now medicine is looking at the other direction to evaluate how positive experiences increases immune system functioning—for example, how exercise strengthens the heart or how faith improves one's blood chemistry.

In fact, Herbert Benson, a cardiologist at Harvard Medical School and Director of the Body/Mind Clinic at the Boston Deaconess Hospital, is investigating the effects of what he calls the "relaxation response," a method of preventative medicine. He points out that prayer was prescribed in early Christian times (codified at Mount Athos in the fourteenth century). A Christian was to pray two times daily, sitting quitely, pay attention to breathing, and say silently, "Lord, Jesus Christ, have mercy upon me, a sinner." In addition to its spiritual value, this method of prayer meets the criteria for effecting the relaxation response, which controls hypertension and the development of other diseases. Where modern man may pay as much as $500 on a course to learn the relaxation response, its physiological benefits can be a natural by-product of following this basic tenet of Christianity.

Benson has demonstrated prayer's scientific benefits for health, yet one wonders what other biological advantages might be revealed were research to be done on other elements of prayer and church life.

Until recently, religious practices often had been looked upon as highly suspect by medical practitioners. By discussing the effects of faith upon healing as anecdotal or similar to the "placebo effect," medicine has discounted the validity of "faith healing." However, the placebo effect has gained increasing respectability today. Although it is still not well understood, scientists theorize that thinking or believing positively activates the cerebral cortex which turns on the endocrine system and adrenal glands. As we come to understand the relationship between mind and body more clearly, I believe that a new, more respectful language for phenomena attributed to the placebo effect will be developed and that medicine will also seek to understand the roles of psychological and spiritual experience upon physiological processes.

Studies reported by the Center for Disease Control have shown that as many as 90% of their patients have self-limiting disorders that are within the range of the body's healing power. As a result, most physicians today are being trained how to allow the body to be its own apothecary, because the most successful prescriptions are those filled by the body itself. The role that one's attitudes, faith, and thought patterns plan in a person's health is important in this direction of medical care.

B. In the Field of Psychology

Psychologists are spearheading studies in psychopharmacology, psychoneuroimmunology, and neuro-psychology (in effect, the self-healing methods of medicine) that might explain, for example, the component of "love" (in effect, the professed purpose of man's religion) as an essential element for emotional stability.

An example of how the disciplines may interface on the subject of "love" may be seen in this way: Catecholamines, which produce a natural stimulant in a person, can be triggered in the body through the following very different sources: by running, a physical activity; by eating chocolate, an ingested food; and by being in love, a relational (psycho-spiritual) phenomenon. These three all produce catecholamines, which create a feeling of euphoria. No doubt the catecholamines explain the so-called runner's high, why we like chocolate and how love makes people feel tireless and exhilarated. I usually advise my psychology students to avoid running, eating chocolate, and being in love at the same time, lest they experience a psychotic episode!

From this example, we can see that the subject of love provides an excellent point for the convergence of medical, psychological, and religious views. Love is the intended by-product of faith in Christ. Scientists now tell us that people who are in love become less tired as a result of reduced levels of lactic acid in their blood. They are also subject to less pain because of the euphoric release of endorphins in their bodies. We also learn that the state of being in love produces more white blood cells, which fight infection, leading to better health. Most importantly, love makes life feel worth living. Consequently, love increases quality of life and the likelihood that physical healing can take place.

Research in this area is indeed fascinating. Harvard psychologist Dr. David McClelland has demonstrated how the immune system can be affected by what one thinks, believes, and feels. In a study of West Point cadets, Immunoglobulin A (S-Ig A), which is essential for a healthy immune system, was measured in a random sample of cadets. McClelland presented three vignettes to the students. In the first instance, the cadets were told that they would be in combat and that they would lose. In the second scenario, the cadets were told that they would be in the battle, but would win. In the third story, the cadets were simply told to watch a video of Mother Theresa of Calcutta. McClelland's findings were that the cadets who were told that they would be in a battle and lose had a weakening of S-Ig A. Cadets who were told that they would be in battle and would win also had an impairment of S-Ig A, though less significant than that of the first group. The cadets who were shown the film of Mother Theresa's selfless love increased their S-Ig A significantly. Such results have encouraged psychologists to focus on religious-oriented themes, such as trust, faith, and hope to better understand human experiences.

C. In the Field of Religion

As stated earlier, Christian theologians and clergy have emphasized for centuries that a person's psychosomatic nature is a principle of life. Today, various faiths have worked to demonstrate their interest in the basic and social sciences—for example, in pastoral care and counseling. There is receptivity in theological studies to show how the tenets of faith affect the healing of lives and how understanding the process or action of faith and healing promotes spiritual, emotional and physical well-being.

So it seems that the disciplines have come full circle. If this is the fortunate case—and we are once more actually approaching the human person as he or she truly is—as a whole person—how do we apply this interdisciplinary perspective to the person who is being served? Are we, the caregivers, prepared to facilitate the healing of the whole person?

Today, a quiet revolution is evolving in the area of healing and health. Often called "holistic" medicine, the thrust of the movement treats an individual as a unity of body, mind, and soul. Illness and health are therefore looked upon in terms of their multidimensional qualities. Holistic medicine considers the close connection between a person's sense of well-being, or lack of it, and health and disease. An individual's biological make-up and his or her personality and spiritual orientation are deemed critical to his of her illness, healing, and growth.

What has been learned from research to support this direction of interest is inviting. A report of the Center of Disease Control shows that lifestyle is nearly 300% more a factor in the cause of death than is human biology. The report goes on to implicate lifestyles and the environment over human biology as the *cause* of terminal illness.

In the medical community, the holistic approach to healing replaces a mechanical or entirely biochemical paradigm of the person. Where in past times medicine would call upon the so-called "ancillary services" of psychology and religion only as a supportive or last resort, now the three fields can be found to work in concert, identifying their unique contribution in the healing process.

In the psychological community, practitioners are beginning to be released from the limitations inherent in animalistic and mechanical assumptions that were previously employed to explain human nature. The American Psychological Association has adapted mandates for both health psychology and transpersonal psychology.

And in the religious community, theologians and priests are beginning to free healing from the bonds of historical, educational, and ritualistic orientations alone, where it typically "speaks about what was done," in the interest of experiencing directly the power of God's presence in a human life.

II. SPIRITUALITY AND HEALING

The foregoing description of the current move toward a holistic approach to healing makes the ground fertile for consideration of the role of spirituality and healing. This is a good time to *ask*, to *wonder*, to *discover* how Christians may bring their talents and their faith to the healing process in order to be whole themselves and to serve as vehicles for healing others.

Richard R. Niebuhr, in his book *Experiencing Religion*, states, "Many explain that modern man cannot believe in miracles; it is not that modern man cannot believe in miracles. It is just that he needs to be shown how."

Enough has been said by physicians and psychologists who advocate the necessity for whole health or by theologians who proclaim that we must approach a synthesis or psychosomatic approach. Rather than setting the table once more with regard to what should be done, let us, with God's grace, endeavor to bring together the fascinating power and range of energies and talents with which we have been endowed to help others.

Our epistemology—our approach to Truth as Christians—affirms that knowledge is a spiritual activity of inner illumination and find no dichotomy between reason and spiritual reality. At the same time, our tradition is opposed to the limitations of idealism and spiritualism—as well as to empiricism—because these approaches are limited—cut off from the full picture—by their own definitions, which are locked into the realms of ideas or matter.

Interestingly, the Fathers of the Church emphasize the positive value of reason. Knowledge, however, means more than being intellectual to the Fathers: It is moral, affective, experiential, ontological, and in agreement with nature. These qualities are critical for a Christian spiritual approach to healing.

Through our *particular educations*, we have become the so-called miracle workers of the disciplines of medicine, psychology, and religion. The ways of the disciplines have often been affected, however, by systems of thought that are not only foreign to the interest of the whole person, but also sometimes alien to the experience of a living spirituality. Whether this problem is exerted through the scientific method of the pure sciences, through the philosophical assumptions underpinning psychological theories, or through the scholasticism implanted in the structure of theological schools, our preparation often leaves us at a loss, if you will, for "showing modern man how to believe in miracles."

History indicates that Byzantine peoples when ill sought healing through individuals whom they felt were holy. Actual healing of ailments is reported through such religious practices as: 1) praying; 2) touching the coffin or relics of a saint; 3) anointing; 4) holy water; 5) incubation (spending the night in a church); and 6) burning tiny pieces of cloth from a saint's garments and inhaling the scent.

Today it seems that we have not only distanced ourselves from the actions associated with being saints but even from faithfully participating in such experiences of healing encounters. Consequently, our lives may be deprived of their spiritual resources and dimensions.

Today, we need to reflect not only on how this affects those entrusted to our care but also on how it affects the modern day healer in his or her life.

What does the surgeon do when not sure if a liver transplant will be rejected?

What does the psychologist tell his patient who says, "I've had a year of radiation, chemo and endless tests. I'm tired of it. I'd rather die."

What does the priest say when a mother arrives on a scene after her four-year old child has been killed in a traffic accident and exclaims. "Why does God punish me? Nicky is so good. Father, it's not fair!"

Should the professional turn to his or her treatment plan alone? Should he or she refer the patient to others? Does he or she play God? Or should the professional call upon God—as did Jesus and Peter—and ask for a miracle? Does not a Christian approach to healing require us to care for others through the vision of God working through us—within us—rather than on our terms alone?

The following personal story illustrates my conjecture. More than ten years ago, my mother discovered a cyst on her breast that was evaluated as benign by three different physicians. After pre-surgical examination, a young surgeon shared his impression that the growth was, in fact, malignant.

A tide of fear came over my mother that by the next day she was so frightened that she did not want to leave her room. I decided to go to Chicago to be with her during the surgery. When I arrived at the hospital, I found my mother very much at ease. After they took her into surgery, I asked what had brought about the change. I learned that the same young surgeon who had delivered the alarming news had stopped by the next day and observed my mother's distress. He took her hands and my sister's hands and prayed to God that my mother be restored and released from the bounds of illness. He prayed for more than one hour! His commitment and conviction were so transparent that both my mother's and sister's spirits were changed. A Roman Catholic woman in the next bed who was suffering from cancer and had been depressed had heard the prayer. Even though her faith in her own religion had lapsed, she felt renewed. The doctor's spirituality gave all of them the perspective and hope to confront what was seemingly insurmountable—not to mention what it did for them physically.

Is not personal conviction of faith a critical part of healing?

III. HEALING AS SPIRITUALITY

The subject of healing and spirituality invites us to a critical, creative, difficult, and immensely important and fulfilling task. The question is not only one of integration, but also an invitation for spiritual renewal and re-awakening. The concern of healing and spirituality is not only a call for holistic health but also a challenge to produce the fruits of this labor—such as fellowships of healers, clinics, services to the needy, and missions.

Therefore, we see that the field of religion alone should not be the only discipline concerned with man's spiritual or supernatural dimensions but that other disciplines have a legitimate role to address "spiritual things." Medicine and psychology are beginning to recognize that their work is enhanced by investigating spiritual issues. At the same time, it is clear that spiritual healing does not have the same focus as medicine and psychology. For its perspective, which has not evolved from the scientific method, does not refer only to what one is, but to what one can be.

The expression "holistic health" often conjures up "far out" approaches to cure ills. We are clearly uninterested in these types of approaches. What we seek are solid methods for a discipline based upon the Christian faith that enable us to be spiritually enlightened helpers. In order to heal others as Christians, we, like the Fathers, need to be alive in "kerygmatic theology," a deeply personal commitment to faith, where, as believers in the Truth of Jesus Christ and the New Testament, we approach our healing task. For clearly even the discipline of religion is not effective in healing if it expresses religiosity and reflects limp faith, nor are the disciplines of the sciences really able to help the whole person if they look upon God as an obscure ghost.

It is suggested that we identify how the various healing methods together combined with spirituality assist both the caregiver and the one that is to be healed. Such an approach is founded upon love, commitment, and the experience of Jesus Christ, as well as competency in one's professional field.

Our Lord tells us, "The Truth will set you free." In the final analysis, I do not believe that there are essential conflicts among those who approach healing from different disciplines, rather that there are different approaches to Truth and knowing. I believe that the eyes of faith afford openness to the knowledge gained in various disciplines and that by definition what is true does not conflict with the truth of God. The challenge for us, however, is to clarify how the various ways of knowing may work together and make us whole.

When scientific healing and faith healing are integrated in our lives we are made whole. Two doctors of the church provide insight on the subject: St. Gregory of Nyssa says, "Health is a blessing for man but man is not happy simply from knowing what health is. He must also possess it." And St. Basil delineates two aspects of knowing: 1) sensorial-intellectual knowledge, which is philosophical; and 2) extra-sensorial knowledge, which is ethical and experiential. Our efforts at healing have all too often focused on the former. As Christians who hear God's call, we are charged not only to hear the latter but to do it.

The Interface of Medicine and Religion

Demetrios J. Constantelos

The term *interface* is subject to several definitions, including the one that calls it "the facts, problems, considerations, theories, and practices shared by two or more disciplines or fields of study." Medicine and religion have much in common. Throughout history their alliance has been intimate and their concerns have often overlapped. The well-being of the human person has been the central objective of both disciplines.

In this essay I will focus more on the historical precedents concerning the relationship between medicine and religion than on the ways and means for their cooperation in the future. The examples of historical precedents will be drawn from the ancient Greek and the Christian Greek Orthodox experience. There are some striking similarities between the two Greek worlds that illustrate not only a persistent continuity from one to the other but also similar responses of the human in times of crisis.

Medicine was described by the ancient Greeks as the *philanthropotate ton epistemon*—the most philanthropic of the sciences—and religion (*threskeia*) was perceived as the instinctive quest of the human being for the divine. As little birds instinctively open their mouths for food, human beings instinctively turn toward their gods, to paraphrase Homer. Religion and medicine were accepted as gifts of divine origin.

It is well known, of course, that medicine and religion have been catalysts in

13

the history of humanity from remote antiquity to recent years. In ancient Greece, religion was constantly searching, evolving, going through several stages of evolution, from anthropomorphic polytheism to philosophical monotheism to ethical Christian monotheism. Medicine was linked to religion under the patronage of the god Asklepios, "for even this branch of learning had to be under the tutelage of something divine," writes in the first century Kornutos of Leptis. But Asklepios was a *theios aner*, a god-man, who could converse using the languages of both divinity and humanity and who could empathize with the human situation to heal and to save. For this reason, Asklepios was the chief antagonist of Christ in the early Christian centuries. In Asklepios, physicians had a divine prototype of love and concern for the human being. Whether directly or indirectly, Asklepios's intervention in human affairs abounds in ancient Greek and Latin literature.[1]

Throughout antiquity, Greek society recognized the human need for divine solicitude for humanity's infirmities. The individual in need of cure would take the initiative and turn to Asklepios and, subsequently, to Asklepios's physician-priest, the Asklepiadae, to perform the cure.

The cult of Asklepios became very popular in the Greco-Roman world of late antiquity, before and after the Christian era. Its purpose was to work a renewal in the human being and a rebirth in health. Some modern medical terms, such as *clinic*, h*ygiene, panacea*, and *iasis*, have their roots in the theories and practices of the Asklepios cult. The first principle of the Asklepios method was to put a patient on a *kline* (bed) in the Asklepios temple. Our term *clinic* derives from *kataklinein*, laying the patient down on a bed. During the night Asklepios would appear to the patient as a tall, bearded man with a white *chiton* (a cloak much like a modern physician's) and a serpent staff (the modern physician's emblem). He was often accompanied by his consort *Hygieia* (health—whence our term hygiene) and his daughters *Panakeia* (thus our *Panacea*—medicine for all diseases) and *Iaso* (whence our *iasis*—the process or condition of healing).

Literary, epigraphic, and archaeological evidence reveal that there were numerous case histories of healed persons from major sanctuaries, such as Epidauros, Kos, Messene, Pergamum, Mytilene, Athens, Aegina, the Tiber Island at Rome, and other Asklepieia.[2] In every case, the cure was considered a mystery, and the rites and methods leading to the cure remind us of rituals and practices in the Christian tradition. The practice of incubation in Asklepios's temple, the pro-

---

[1]*See* Emma J. Edelstein and Ludwig Edelstein, Asclepius, 2 vols. (Baltimore, 1945. Reprinted New York, 1975), 1:180. Volume 1 contains a collection of texts and references to Askelepios's life and deeds, his cult, as well as images and temples. Volume 2 presents an analysis of the material assembled.

[2]*Ibid.*, p. 36-59. *See also* Guido Majno, *The Healing Hand* (Cambridge, MA, 1975), 201-205, and W. K. Guthrie, *The Greeks and their Gods* (Boston, MA, 1955), 242-253; cf. E. R. Dodds, *The Greeks and the Irrational* (Los Angeles, CA, 1971), 110-119.

nouncement of Asklepios's sacred words (*hieroi logoi*), and the belief that both *soma kai psyche* (body and soul) are restored to harmony have been assimilated into Christianity.

Each case at the sanctuaries was different, and the personal relationship between the divinity and the patient was emphasized. Every cure presupposed the presence of certain central principles, some of which were spiritual and some pragmatic: the ritual of incubation, which may be described as total surrender to God's providence and will; faith in the possibility of cure; and also dietetic and therapeutic methods, such as baths and exercises.

It was the responsibility of the patient to take the initiative and visit his physician. Whether one was ill from arthritis, epiphysis, rheuma, crisis, asthma, tetanos, anthrax, opisthotonos, mesocolon, dysenteria, pleuritis, hypochondria, a wound or any other of several other illnesses mentioned in the Hippocratic books, one would turn first to a physician—the representative of *physis*—the physical. It was though that the physical, without instruction or knowledge, did what was necessary. Nature was considered the physician of diseases, but when the physical failed and no physician was able to heal, the patient lost no hope. He or she would turn to the metaphysical—beyond the physical to God.

Asklepios, the patron god of physicians, would heal either directly or through a physician. The patient would pray to Asklepios, and the physician would lend a hand. "Prayer indeed is good, but while calling on the gods one must oneself lend a hand," as we read in a Hippocratic book.[3] Direct healing was performed in the Asklepieion—the temple of Asklepios. The patient was taken to the temple, where he was required to lie down in the sacred hall called the *abation*, the "innermost chamber" or *sanctum sanctorum*, and wait for the god to appear and either heal directly or give advice in a dream. It was a halfway encounter of the patient with God—with healing itself. Here are a few cases copied from a large marble *stele* found in the celebrated Asklepieion in Epidauros:

> Gorgias of Herakleia with pus in a battle he had been wounded by an arrow in the lung and for a year and a half he had suppurated so badly that he filled sixty-seven basins with pus. While sleeping in the temple he saw a vision. It seemed to him the god extracted the arrowhead from his lung. When day came he walked out well holding the arrowhead in his hands.

When Asklepios used a drug, it was a drug that induced dreams. Here is an illustration:

> Timon was wounded by a spear under his eye. While sleeping in the temple he saw a dream. It seemed to him that the God rubbed down an herb

---

[3]Hippocrates, "Peri Diaites," W. H. S. Jones, ed. *Hippocrates*, 4 vols. (Cambridge, MA, 1967), 4-298.

and poured it into his eye and he became well.

Asklepios even practiced dream surgery, as illustrated in the following story concerning the eyes of Anticrates of Onidos:

> In a battle [Anticrates] had been hit by a spear in both eyes and had become blind and the spearpoint he carried with him sticking in his face. While sleeping he saw a vision. It seemed to him that the god pulled out the middle and then fitted into his eyelids again the so-called pupils. When day came he walked out sound.[4]

Because of his healing and philanthropic concerns, Asklepios was called Soter and Philanthropos, epithets widely used in Christian and Orthodox hymnography for Christ. The Asklepieia were the forerunners of Christian hospitals.

It is an acknowledged fact that Christianity did not seek to destroy the past but instead to consecrate it. In its process of dissemination, Christianity adopted and absorbed much of the culture of the pagan past. Christianity did not destroy the pagan past. In the Christian Orthodox tradition, there has been no antagonism between medicine as a pagan inheritance and religious faith, between science and belief, between reason and creed, and between faith and culture. Indeed, the striking persistence of ancient Greek though and pagan images and practices up to the present day serve as a reminder that Christian theology and art by no means obliterated the Greco-Roman heritage.

In the history of Christian Hellenism, we discern attitudes similar to those that existed in Pagan Hellenism. In both chronological periods, medicine was viewed as a god-given gift for the benefit of humankind. Throughout the Byzantine era, in which Orthodox Christianity formulated many of its present doctrines, ethical teachings, and forms of worship, medicine and religion became catalysts in the daily life and civilization of the people.

Orthodox Christianity assumed a positive stand toward medicine precisely because it had adopted the Greek mind, which remained one of its permanent categories. The teachings about medicine and religion of both Hippocrates and Galenos did not contradict any basic doctrines of Christian Orthodoxy. Hippocrates's recognition that an individual's constitution determines the nature of certain diseases and his emphasis on the sacredness and the healing powers of nature made him a source of reference throughout the Byzantine era. "Holy will I keep my life and my art" reads the Hippocratic oath.[5] Hippocrates harmonized rational Greek inquiry with religious faith.

Galenos excelled in diagnosis and prognosis in physiology and anatomy,

---

[4]Majno, *op.cit.*, 201-203.
[5]Hippocrates, "Orkos," W. H. S. Jones, ed. *Hippocrates*, 1:298.

which he advanced through experimentation. But it was his reverence for the human person, his ardent belief in the divinity ("everything manifests god's glory," he writes) and his religious attitude toward ailing persons that contributed to the cultivation of a positive alliance between medical science and religious faith. Orthodox Christianity, unlike its Western counterpart, did not have to rediscover the value of scientific medicine because it had never left its native land and it preserved the high conception of the art of healing of the ancient masters.[6]

History confirms that many rites and liturgical terms of the Christian Church were adopted from the religious beliefs, practices, and ceremonies of the people who in adopting Christianity, changed little of their faith and culture. *Soter* (savior), *Philanthropos* (lover of the human being), *poliouchos* (protector of the city), *patroos* (fatherly), *mysterion* (mystery), *hiereus* (priest), *thysia* (sacrifice), *analepsis* (ascension), *panegyris* (festival), *hierokeryx* (preacher), *ekklesia* (church), *naos* (temple), *myesis* (initiation), *pannychis* (night service), *thymiamata* (incense), *koimeterion* (cemetery)[7] and many more religious terms in current use in the Greek and other Eastern Orthodox Churches reveal the unbroken continuity between pagan and Christian culture, between non-Christian and Christian Hellenism.

The practice of *incubation*, or sleeping in the Church or at the feet of icons and votives of legs, arms, or other parts of the body dedicated to icons of "Christos" or the "Panagia Parthena," remind us of similar models hanging in temples of Asklepios. Whether in Greek and Roman antiquity, in the Christian Middle Ages, or in Modern times, people feel the need for a touch of the *paionios cheir* (divine hand) for the restoration of health.

There is nothing wrong with this heritage. Who shall say whether these customs are blasphemous and irrational, "pagan" or "Christian"? Christians, who have inherited a mass of customs directly derived from the thought and the ritual of the Greek healing god Asklepios, need not apologize for this inheritance. In the last analysis, these customs are neither pagan nor Christian. They are intensely human and universal, an utterance of the helplessness of persons in affliction and pain crying out for the aid of a power beyond themselves and their fellow human beings, whether physicians or priests, for hope, certainty, and health realized.[8]

Purity of body, faith, prayer, and especially love of human beings were prerequisites for effective healing. Hippocrates writes, "Where there is love of the human being there is also love of the medical art." The term *philanthropia*, in the sense of love for the human being, *philein ton anthropon*, was widely used in

---

[6]D. J. Constantelos, "Medicine, Byzantine" in *Dictionary of the Middle Ages*, Joseph R. Strayer, ed., vol. 8 (New York, 1987), 244-246.

[7]For these terms in the Asklepios's cult, *see* Alice Walton, *Asklepios: The Cult of the Greek God of Medicine* (Ithaca, 1894. Reprinted Chicago, 1974), esp. 47-56.

[8]*Ibid.*, 76-77.

Byzantine writings, including theological and medical literature. And religion and medicine were both concerned with the health of the whole human being; Church and Medicine received the human being as psychosomatic entity.

Notwithstanding the skepticism of some conservative monks, who questioned the efficiency of medicine and emphasized the effectiveness of "holy men" rather than physicians in the cure of illnesses, the Orthodox Church has never doubted the usefulness of medicine. It has been rightly observed by specialists that in no other scientific field is the Byzantine contribution greater than in medicine. Several major Church Fathers not only studied medicine but also made important contributions in the area of health and health services—from the fourth down to recent centuries. Basil the Great, the founder of the first major hospital of the Middle Ages, Eusebios of Caesarea, Nemesios of Emesa, John Eleemon, Pausikakos of Apameia, Photios, and others described epidemics such as smallpox and diphtheria and made important contributions to clinical medicine and physiology, including a description of the nervous system. Many churchmen trained in both theology and medicine used their medical knowledge in establishing hospitals, leprosaria, and other philanthropic institutions. Indeed, the emergence of the clinic and the hospital proper was the result of the Greek Church's positive attitude toward medicine.

There was no monolithic attitude toward the cause of disease. Some Church Fathers and Christian lay physicians viewed illness as punishment sent by the divinity; others felt that it had natural causes, such as food, work, climate, and environmental factors. While some physicians—clergyman and laypersons alike—and patients made a rational analysis of a disease and sought a logical and natural therapeutic approach, others confused the logical with superstition and the rational with the irrational. Diet, baths, exercises and drugs were all prescribed and an emphasis was placed on religious faith, incubation of the patient in the church, the service of the Euchelaion (Holy Unction), and other religious formulas. The Hospital and the Church cooperated closely in the task of restoring the ill to a healthy society. Hospitals were built next to churches, and all hospitals had chapels for services and prayer.[9]

The close relationship between religion and medicine in the Orthodox tradition is further attested to by the existence of many physician-priests as was the case in Greek antiquity. Throughout the Byzantine era, many monks, priests, bishops, and patriarchs received a medical education and practiced the profession, as did the popular healing saints, such as Therapon, Panteleimon, Kosmas, Damianos, Kyros, Sampson, and Diomedes, whose names are cited even today in the Orthodox Church services. Many physicians, who were also ordained clergymen, were highly respected. They were expected to be experts and practice the act of healing on both "bodies and souls." In addition to Pausikakos mentioned earlier, the Patriarchs Politianos, Eutychios, Kyrillos II, Nicholas II, Meletios Pegas, all of

---

[9]Demetrios J. Constantelos, *Byzantine Philanthropy and Social Welfare* (New Brunswick, NJ, 1968), 152-184, esp. 175-177.

Alexandria; Anastasios from Tralleis, Andronikos the deacon, and Gerontios of Nicomedia are but a few of the many physicians ordained as priests, serving the needs of bodies and souls.[10]

The same practice survived until recent years, as I illustrate by the following examples from the Greek experience.

The name of several prominent physicians who studied theology are known. These were ordained priests and played leading roles in the life of post-Byzantine Greece. In the eighteenth century, a physician named Parthenios Petrakis became a monk, subsequently received ordination, and founded a monastery which carries his name to the present—Mone Petraki. The physician-priest Petrakis established his medical practices there for all Athenians who needed his services. After his death, the *iatrophilosophos* (physician-philosopher) Dionysiod Pyrros was ordained a priest and, in cooperation with the hegoumenos of the Petraki Monasteri, established the first scientific school of modern Greece in 1812. He taught medicine, pharmacology, hygiene, botany, and related sciences. It is interesting to note that in 1835 he was elected the first president of the Medical Society of Modern Greece.[11]

Throughout the history of Orthodox Christianity, medicine was used as a rule, not as a safeguard against demonic powers, to prevent evil influences, or to propitiate the divinity (as in primitive or underdeveloped societies), but as an experiential science in the Aristotelian tradition. The Aristotelian philosophy of science, which from as early as the thirteenth century dominated medical science in Western European universities, especially the University of Padua, never deserted its native ground. Thanks to the Orthodox understanding of the cosmos, medicine found a ready association with religion.

The thirteenth century of our era marked a turning point in the alliance between medicine and religion. Medical studies were pursued with far greater vigor with the propensity for innovation than they had been before. Physicians were respected and valued, and hospitals and medical services were perceived as the deepest possible expression of love and concern for the human being. Anti-medical sentiment was very limited and rather rhetorical. It had its source in isolated monastic circles and heretical movements. The mainstream of religious thought considered medicine proof of God's philanthropy and of the goodness of creation. Of course, this attitude does not mean that there was no criticism of physicians themselves. Patients complained then as they complain today that physician were paid exorbitant fees. It should be noted, however, that physicians' high fees, their failure to cure medical problems, and their reputation for cupidity is a *topos* in both hagiog-

---

[10]Demetrios J. Constantelos, "Clerics and Secular Professions in the Byzantine Church," *Byzantina*, vol. 13 (1985), 373-390, esp. 382-388.

[11]Chrysostomos Roumeliotes, "E Prosphora tou Orthodoxou Monachismou," *Ekklesia*, vol. 64.1 (Athens, 1987), 404.

raphy and various descriptions of miracles.[12]

In any case, it was under these circumstances that the faithful would turn from the physical—the physician—to the metaphysical—to Christ, who is described in the Liturgy as "the physician of bodies and souls" and to divine intervention through liturgical services, sacramental acts, relics, and intercessions of holy persons.

Miraculous cures, whether legendary or real, abound in the *Lives of Saints*. The following illustrations came from the miracles attributed to Athanasios, a fourteenth-century saint and former Patriarch of Constantinople:

> Meletios Poteras, of Medeia, fell victim to a terrible evil spirit, which did not simply possess him for several years, but filled his soul with terror and darkness and treated him despitefully in every way. . . . He used to collapse frequently and fall down and suffered all "the ills" of men possessed by spirits: spasms, convulsions, attacks of dizziness. . . .
>
> . . . Meletios, disregarding all human assistance, sought refuge in God and His servant came to the sanctuary where the precious coffin of Athanasios lies; he fell before it in supplication and bathed it in warm tears. Then Meletios made use of the drug which wards off evil spirits and all suffering, being truly the oil of mercy; he blended it with prayers and tears and straightway was freed from his demonic possession [epilepsy?].

Note that is was after Meletios had despaired of medical assistance that he sought the intercession of the saint. He prayed first, and then he used the drug. Human assistance and divine help, prayer, drug, and healing was the process by which Meletios cured.

The case of Ioannis Vliangenos, who suffered from a similar illness, reminds one of the incubation and dream therapies of the Asklepieia. He sought refuge to the church where Athanasios' coffin was laid. While in deep sleep, the saint appeared to him in his sleep, took hold of his head, and bade him open his mouth. Then he said, "Behold you have been freed from the evil spirit; now that you have found salvation through your faith, depart in peace. . . . As soon as Vlangenos awoke, he was liberated from the evil spirit." Once again, despairing of help, Ioannis Vlangenos sought assistance from the Church. The recovery of his faith made him well through the intervention of the Saint.[13]

---

[12]Alice-Mary M. Talbot, *Faith Healing in Late Byzantium* (Brookline, MA, 1983), 132; Halina Evert-Kappesowa, "The Social Rank of a Physician in the Early Byzantine Empire," *Byzance et les Slaves: Etudes de civilization* (Paris, 1979), 145.

[13]Talbot, *op. cit.*, 78-79.

In addition to medicine, the intercession of holy persons, and special services in the last centuries of the Byzantine era, the Church officially adopted a sacrament of healing. Even though belief in the miraculous was always present in the experience of the Church, it was after the thirteenth century that the Sacrament of Holy Unction was officially adopted as the sacrament to be administered for the healing of illnesses of body and soul, with emphasis on physical healing. Parenthetically, it is interesting to note that at the Council of Lyons (1274), which aimed to unify the Western and Eastern churches, the Greek delegation was asked to explain the doctrines of its Church. It responded by saying repeatedly that the Sacrament of the Euchelaion was administered only to sick people for the restoration of their health. In fact the Greek Father criticized the Latin Church for administering the Sacrament as a last rite.[14] Because of the interrelationship between the body and the soul, the Sacrament was dispensed with for the forgiveness of sins and for the healing of the soul and the mind. "Great are the benefits of this rite upon both soul and body" advised Saint Symeon, Archbishop of Thessalonike (1410-1429).[15] It is well known that the Church today, through its many special services and prayers, is deeply concerned with the psychosomatic well-being of its members. Indeed, one of its many characteristics is that the Church's liturgical life has embraced the totality of the cosmos and all of humanity's spiritual and physical needs. From the moment of birth to the moment of departure from this life; for a single personal object to a public project; for the installation of the village mayor to the inauguration of the president of the Republic—for every occasion and every need the Church is in attendance encouraging, educating, sanctifying.[16]

The Orthodox Church sees the human person as a *synergo theou*, a collaborator with God, because of his affinity with God. The human being is primarily a soul, a mind, a spirit with a body—not a body with a spirit. Thus, the emphasis is on the spirit—the mind and soul over the body. Faith as a factor in the healing process, the belief that "everything is possible to those who believe," faith as a surrendering of mind and body to the Creator's providence are teachings that are integrated in the belief system of the Orthodox.[17]

But Orthodoxy means more than faith alone; it also means a way of life, a culture, an all-embracing cosmic-view that sees a harmonious union between the physical and the metaphysical, body and soul. It is the organic character of the body and soul union that makes the alliance of medicine and religious faith mean-

---

[14]A. Theiner and F. Miklosich, *Monumenta spectantia ad unionem ecclesiarum Graecae et Romanae* (Vienna, 1872), 27-28.

[15]Symeon of Thessalonike, "Peri tes teletes tou Hagiou Elaiou," in *Symeon Archiepiskopou Thessalonikes Ta Apanta* (Thessalonike, no date. Reprinted from the 1882 ed.), 228.

[16]The *Mega Euchologion* includes not only the Sacramental services but also many brief rites and prayers for practically every occasion of man's life.

[17]Mat. 8:13, 21:22; Mark 9:23; Lk. 8:50. *See also* Leonidas J. Philippides, *E Pistis os paragon vevaias iaseos* (Athens, 1947), esp. 19-30.

ingful and indeed necessary. Orthodoxy is radically opposed to any dualistic interpretation of the human being and to any view that identifies the earth life with evil
and sees illness as the result of the demonic. Orthodoxy's God is a *Philanthropos
Theos*, the source of a beautiful and orderly cosmos—not a life-hating Devil.[18]

Modern trends in religious faith and health sciences relationships in the
Orthodox world are not meant to be a return to the past or an escape to the ancient
Greek Asklepieia or medieval Byzantine *nosokomeia* (hospitals) but a response to
existential needs, even a reaction to a secularized and commercialized medicine.
Health is no longer viewed as the absence of sickness but the realization of human
potential when the human realizes God's kingdom "in us" and His presence
"inside" us. Indeed "in God we live and move and have our being," as the ancient
Greek poet put it and St. Paul confirmed it (Acts 17:28). In the light of this vision
of God, Orthodox Christian physicians should have no problem accepting the
ministry of healing either through the Sacrament of Holy Unction or other forms of
liturgical prayers and services. It should be noted that the ministry of healing discussed here is not the television-style "faith healing" that denies the value of scientific medicine. The Ministry of Healing is not self-sufficient, acknowledges its
limitations, and cooperates with medicine.

However, is not modern medicine dominated by the rationalists and agnostics?
Is it not irrational and unscientific to believe in a ministry of healing? Before re-
flecting on these questions, let us consider an additional question: What is faith and
what is healing? "Faith is the assurance of things hoped for, the conviction of
things not seen" (Hebr. 11:1). In the context of this definition, even rationalist and
skeptics should admit that faith is very much a major factor in the process of healing.

Every patient needs the reassurance of things hoped for—that is, healing—and
the conviction of things not seen but soon to be realized—such as the return of an
injured or damaged part of the human body to its natural and normal state of being
to the extent that it is possible. Faith as an attitude of the mind possesses tremendous powers. If properly utilized the mind could undermine and even defeat illness, as well as enhance the health of the body, spirit and emotions. We are told
that physicians and other scientists who use new tools of brain physiology in order
to check out the mind and its powers are no longer a small group of wishful
thinkers.

It is widely accepted that negative emotions and attitudes are detrimental to
health while controlled emotions and positive thinking contribute to the develop-

---

[18]For an excellent understanding of Christian Orthodox anthropology within
the context of theology, *see* Elias Mastrogianropoulos, *Oi Pateres tes Ekklesias kai
o anthropos* (Athens, 1966), esp. 71-285, and Paul Evdokimov, *L'Orthodoxie*
(Paris, 1959), Part 1; Greek translation by A. T. Mourtzopoulos, *E Orthodoxia*
(Thessalonike, 1972), 56-61.

ment of a system immune towards various physical and emotional illnesses. The links between brain and body, belief and immunity has long been recognized. Our ancestors relied more than we on prayer, intuition, and belief. We have added today experiential knowledge to science. The prayers of the Church not only invoke divine intervention, but also provide the ground for certainty, hope, and positive expectations; they strengthen the health system of the patient. In this light, then, one may assert that the means of the Church for healing are not anachronistic but as timely as ever.

In recent years, scientists have accumulated sufficient evidence indicating that thoughts, beliefs, and emotional states can affect one's immune system. To visualize health promoting images, such as God's touch healing the sick; to believe that God's presence in the human being can expel intruders; to accept seriously the commands "Go; be it done for you as you have believed" (Mat. 8:13) and "according to your faith be it done to you" (Mat. 9:29; Mat. 15:28) are positive instruments in religion as well as in medicine and psychology.

The dialogue between medicine, psychology and religion must continue, for many of their elements converge in their interest for the well being of humanity. A critical analysis of the teachings of Orthodox Christianity on the nature and destiny of the human being reveals but little that is antithetical to the pursuits and goals of medicine and psychology. The voice of the Sacrament of Holy Unction and of other liturgical services and prayers is a life-affirming voice, speaking the positive, looking not only for the holiness but also for the wholeness of soul, mind, and body.

The healing approach of Orthodox Christianity is not necessarily the destruction or elimination of illness but the realization of human potential within the dynamics of God's creation.[19] In addition to the prayers for health, Orthodox Christianity also has prayers for the peaceful departure of the ill person from a physical reality into a metaphysical perpetual existence. That is, the voice of the faith is not only life-affirming in time but also life-affirming in eternity. Should the inevitable come in spite of prayers and medical assistance, the patient must surrender to God's spirit in peace and faith. It must be emphasized, however, that whether in matters of life or death the Church only petitions, it does not command it. It only invokes God's intervention and mercy, but it does not dictate God's decision.

Another fruitful meeting-point between religion and medicine today lies in the fact that both accept the recreative power of nature that brings healing. The Church never directly heals anybody. Prayers, services, holy persons, and celebrants are instruments of healing—not healers. Similarly, physicians, surgeons, and psy-

---

[19]*See* Stanley Samuel Harakas, "The Eastern Orthodox Tradition," in *Caring and Curing*, by L. Numbers and Darrel W. Amunden, eds., (New York, 1986), esp. 152-153, 166-167.

chotherapists are not miracle workers and do not directly heal anybody; they seek by their skills and their art to remove obstacles to nature's healing energies, to correct chemical imbalances in the body, or to take away diseased tissue.

The trend in Orthodox Christian thought today is to see scientific medicine and the spiritual dimensions of man's well-being in a holistic perspective. The human being is viewed as the totality of reality, however small—as a microcosm of God's creation in the process of deification by reason of his affinity with God. Soul and body are not two separate entities but the spiritual and physical elements of the same being.[20] Though I possess no prophetic charisma and cannot predict whether this approach will be satisfactory to practitioners of twenty-first century medicine, I profess my personal satisfaction with what can be called modern Christian Orthodox anthropology. It is a well balanced perception of the nature and destiny of the human being.

The present, however, and the twenty-first century have new challenges to and different problems for both medicine and religion. Changing technology has an impact on ethics and traditional values, on parenthood, euthanasia, AIDS, and other ethical issues, such as whether it is permissible to remove support systems and allow patients to expire when the inevitable is apparent; whether pregnancy outside its natural place is morally acceptable; whether undesirable pregnancies should be terminated; whether contagious diseases such as AIDS should make the Church reconsider the method by which the Eucharist is administered.

Notwithstanding the perplexities involved in the interface of medicine and religion today, the alliance between the Orthodox Christian faith and medicine need not be abandoned in the present, and their creative dialogue must be pursued vigorously in the twenty-first century.

---

[20]Harakas, *ibid.*, and Philippides, *op cit.*, 9-10.

Science and Morality: When Technology and Ethics Meet

Bishop Nicholas

The following is the frame of reference that I will use to focus on the relationships between science and morality and technology and ethics:

1) We as Christians are called to respond to the overwhelming medical and psychological issues, options, and developments that appear to face mankind in ever increasing numbers each day. If we remain silent on these issues, our decision to do so will not be seen as a shrewd, intellectual decision in the face of data, much of which is still inconclusive. Rather, our silence surrenders our responsibility to be ready to preach "in season and out of season," as St. Paul counsels Timothy, and to be "ready always to give answer to the hope that is in you." Our silence, rather than testifying to our wisdom, would convict us of the grossest spiritual ignorance.

2) If we do not respond as Orthodox Christians to the issues before us, it would be foolhardy for us to believe that they would remain unaddressed. Rather, the "world" will respond—unchallenged—and its frame of reference will be drawn from the secular rather than the sacred sciences.

   Our surrender would not be to a faceless, morally neutral world, but one like that described by St. Isaac the Syrian, when summarizing Scripture and Tradition, as "an inclusive term used by the Lord and the Fathers to refer to the sinful passions preying upon men."

3)   The basis for our response must develop logically from our confession of
     Orthodox Christianity, which includes not only the Word of God entrusted to
     Holy Scripture and Sacred Tradition, but also His Word contained in the on-
     going revelation of the Holy Spirit in the Church and in our lives. Unlike the
     world and its wisdom of ever-changing, often competing, and, at time, plainly
     contradictory theories and explanations, the Word and Its Wisdom remain the
     same—"Jesus Christ, the same yesterday, today and forever" (Hebrews
     13:8)—and are always informative of our human condition: "All Scripture is
     given by inspiration of God and is profitable for doctrine, reproof, for
     correction, for instruction in righteousness" (2 Timothy 3:16).

4)   Our Christianity must be integral to our self-definition, and it must be the
     integrative principle for responding as doctors, psychologists, clergy, or
     laypersons. We are Orthodox Christians first and foremost—Orthodox
     Christians who are also healing practitioners, not healing practitioner who
     happen to be Orthodox. Our identity stems from our incorporation through
     Baptism into the mystical Body of Christ, and all that we do must derive from
     that knowledge. This directionality cannot be reversed. Therefore, Christian
     counsel, Christian response, and Christian decision-making must integrate our
     posture towards the new technologies, human conditions and dilemmas, and
     the exploding sources of information about us.

If this is our frame of reference, let me speak a bit on the context in which it
will be developed. First, to our theme: "Science and Morality: When Technology
and Ethics Meet." What loaded terms! To even attempt to define them could lead
us into an endless abyss, as demonstrated by the historians and philosophers who
chose just such a path. Instead of definition, then, let us look at the grammar of this
title, for linguists have long since taught us that the ways in which we
grammatically structure our universe reflect our cognitive perception of reality and
shape our response to it as well.

Significantly enough, what often impedes us in our Christian call to respond
holistically and in an integrative fashion are not the "nouns" in the conference's
title—*science*, *morality*, *technology*, and *ethics*—but the conjunction, the adverb,
and the verb: that is, the two *ands*, one *when* and one *meet*.

Although *and* usually mean "to add," it also denotes separation—
discontinuity, if you will—between two distinct entities that are necessary but may
be unrelated. For example, physicians often prescribe "Ampicillin three times a
day with plenty of water" for an infection. Both are necessary to be effective.
However, the conjunction *and* also serves as a reminder that *ampicillin* and *water*
are two different substances in empirical reality. The nouns of the conference
theme are related in a similar manner: although the implication is that both *science*
and *morality* help describe each other, the *and* implies a separate, distinct empirical
corpus of knowledge and somewhat begs the issue of one's mutually influencing
the other, or even stronger yet, determining the other.

Now, whereas these distinctions may be true in the narrow sense in which, of necessity, we partition the universe to explain and understand it, there is, in fact, *no* basis in Scripture or Tradition for this polarity of two separate entitles—two distinct bodies of knowledge, so to say. Simply put, there is no spiritual distinction. Rather, we are instructed holistically and told that whether dealing with natural, spiritual, personal, experimental, or intellectual knowledge, each derives from God and each is revelatory. Each is subject to Him for its meaning and content: "The heavens declare the glory of God; and the firmament shows His handiwork," sings out the Divine David (Psalm 19:1). Elaborating on this notion, Solomon declares: "For the Lord gives wisdom, and out of His mouth come knowledge and understanding" (Proverbs 2:6). Paul echoes centuries later: ". . . all the riches of the full assurance of understanding, to the knowledge of the mystery of God, both of the Father and of Christ, in whom are hidden all the treasure of wisdom and understand" (Colossians 2:2-3). Far, then, from being two distinct categories of thought, each derives from God as revelation—the first, science, denoting revelation about the natural order, and the second, morality, denoting revelation about the social order as it is guided by spiritual truths. Both, however, depend on an over-arching spiritual reality for their source and content.

We do not, then, have two distinct bodies of knowledge, but two subsets of Divine Revelation—unified in a single spiritual reality that is *personalized* in Christ and present in His teachings. Though artificially separated by our human thought each has its origin in God as the locus and the measuring stick for evaluating and validating its content.

Now we come to the *when* and *meet* of our theme—an adverb that denotes time and a verb that denotes encounter. We are told that this encounter takes place between the domains of technology and ethics. Once again, however, we must subject this linguistic structuring to Scriptural scrutiny in order to determine if, in fact, we are dealing with two independent bodies of knowledge of two subsets of a common revelation.

We have just seen how the *and* in our analogy functions to stress the disparity between *science* and *morality*. The same is true of *technology* and *ethics*. Once again, however, we are dealing with a distinction that is linguistic rather than Scriptural. Perhaps the clearest demonstration of this fact is in St. Paul's Epistles to the Ephesians and Romans, both of which are classical texts on ethics as a system for setting forth standards of right conduct. In Romans, St. Paul initiates his discussion of proper behavioral choice with words: "Do not be conformed to this world, but be transformed by the renewing of your mind, that you may prove what is that good and acceptable and perfect will of God" (12:2). Everything, then, derives from the will of God as revealed in the teachings of Christ "that he might fill all things," as Paul continues in Ephesians (4:11).

Christ is the origin of all things, in all things, and the Being by whom all things are held together. Whether dealing with science or morality, technology or ethics, all knowledge becomes subject to Him as the single unifying spiritual truth and, by extension, is entrusted to His Church as His mystical body, to define, clarify, develop, discard, or apply.

In attempting to address the specific issues of this paper, we must be clear about the meaning of its theme, which is primarily to discover the spiritual realities that elucidate the empirical subsets of *science* and *morality* and *technology* and *ethics.*

And now a word or two concerning the verb *meet.* It has often been my experience that the information following the colon in a title conveys the major operative information about its theme. So it is, I believe, in this case. It seems obvious—or failing that, not terribly controversial—to posit that *technology* and *ethics* are the behavioral poles of *science* and *morality*, respectively. That is to say, whereas *science* and *morality* denote both the general principles and methodology for discovering truths about the natural and sociological order, *technology* and *ethics* attempt to apply these general principles to specific situations. Thus, for example, we have in theology the polarity between good and evil, expressing itself in the behavioral judgments of right and wrong. In the field of science, we likewise have a general gloss of retrovirus expressing itself in the specific configuration of HIV-T3.

It is significant, then, that we tend to think of the operational arm of morality—that is, ethics—as only meeting science at its operational level of technology rather than in it its parent-terms—science and morality—as they, likewise, derive from the same spiritual truth—Christ and His teachings.

It appears to me that the benefit of this linguistic analysis lies in the following: First, before we process with the specific issues of this paper, it behooves us to make clear the *presuppositions* built into the very wording of our theme itself—albeit unconsciously. These presuppositions relate together as a structure to demonstrate, at a minimum, a tacit acceptance of a dichotomy between science and morality not only on the empirical level of content, but on the ontological level of origin as well. This dichotomy could easily lead us to overlook, or as is more usual, to pay simple lip service to the divine origins of both in the teachings and Person of Christ and His church, rather than grappling with the more difficult problem of unifying a cohesive scientific and moralistic orientation in light of their common origin in higher spiritual truths of the Word of God. Similarly, we can be easily distracted from the task of positing, even as experimental and by trial-and-error, appropriate Christian witnesses in the face of ever-increasing medical and psychological research and discovery.

Second, if we deal primarily with the meeting of science and morality on their operational level of technology and ethics, we can easily overlook the implicit world view inherent in each parent term and inadequately appreciate how this world view evaluates and determines our behavioral—that is, technological or ethical—

responses in particular choice situations, whether these situations occur in the laboratory, the doctor's office, or the marketplace.

Third, insufficient attention paid to both the source of knowledge and the determinants of behavior can often result in failure to develop a consistent, as opposed to a bifurcated, response-to-discovery orientation and its concomitant application-for-action methodology. Simply put: Are we as Orthodox in our mental and behavioral responses as health care professionals as we are in our local Orthodox parishes? Or do we develop and use one set of standards to direct our professional searchings and goals, determine our professional decisions, and evaluate our professional progress and yet another for our spiritual pursuits and achievements? Put yet another way: Do we pray as if all depended upon God but work as if all depends upon us. Failing this either/or hypothesis, we must discover and attempt to synthesize the *where*, *when*, and *how* for the overlapping of our standards of choice and evaluation.

Fourth, failing, first, to attribute adequately the common origin of both scientific and moral knowledge to the revelation of God and, second, to attempt to synthesize our professional and vocational behavior easily leads to a failure to make explicit the principles by which we prioritize our pursuits and evaluate the appropriateness of our behavior. In areas of doubtful congruence between secular discovery and Sacred Truth do we sufficiently recognize that we must let Sacred Truth determine both the direction of our profession and prevail in the judgments of our discoveries, both in their "pure" and in their "applied" meanings.

Before continuing, let me reaffirm that I am acutely sensitive to how the points mentioned above may appear to the modern era as an arcane *apologia* for the establishment of tyrannical theocracy. But this prejudice or bias is precisely what we must guard against. All of us have been so unconsciously affected by the learning process of the universities and the development of secular and humanistic thought that the very idea of subjugating our professionalism to the overlordship of Christ appears as anathema. Wasn't the central issue of Jefferson's message the right of all to pursue knowledge to its end point, to wherever it may lead? Do not even the the historians use such now commonplace appellations as the "Age of Faith" and the "Age of Reason" to demarcate human epochs radically different in their approach to and evaluation of knowledge? Moreover, does not the chronological sequencing of the two epochs posit the gradual evolution and triumph of reason over human faith—a movement of human awareness away from the dark dungeons of superstition and into the clear light of demonstrable certainty—a shift from a primitive and quaint theocentric to a sophisticated and thoroughly modern anthropocentric focus?

Has not the result been twofold: some people have left the Church, convinced of its irrationality or irrelevancy (and, parenthetically, as churchmen we must accept our share of responsibility for this condition); those who remain confessing and communicating Christians have developed *de facto* parallel, non-integrative, and non-integrating value structures—one designed to order their physical/professional universe and the other to order their mental/spiritual universe?

Yes, our Church continues to confess: "All of you who have been baptized into Christ have put on Christ." *All*—not just the bishops and priests, but the lay-professionals as well. *Put on*—not just some of the time and in some circumstance but for all times and all places. If we as Orthodox fully appreciate the true nature of the Church, we need fear neither charges of being arcane nor of being tyrannical. When we realize that we, the clergy and laity together are the Church—the Mystical Body of Christ—we understand that the over the overlordship of Christ not only does not imply, but explicitly forbids, that men and women should act in tyranny to make decisions against the common good. The reason for this prohibition is that the common good is precisely located in the Person of Christ and manifested in his works. The Church as a living body demands that the laity and the clergy participate in a dialogue so that each individual position is openly discused by the Body and is a consequence of prayerful intercession to be accepted or rejected by the Body operating through the agency of the Holy Spirit, who by definition, "leads into all truth." The Church, then, as the Body of Christ—when it has functioned in this Scriptural model—has never been the tyrant of the people out the advocate for and the victory of the people in the search for good over evil and right over wrong, whether in the realm of belief or behavior.

How, then, does what we have just said relate to our original four aims?

First, regarding our calling as Christians to respond to the overwhelming increase in technology applied to a multiplying of human needs: We have the responsibility to participate actively in the direction, content, and evaluation of scientific development and technological implementation by virtue of our very calling as the Royal Priesthood of Christ—the Church—the Body of Believers. We participate in response to Our Lord's great commission as outlined in Matthew: "As you go *preach* the Message, the Kingdom of Heaven is near, *heal* the sick, *raise* the dead, *cleanse* the leper, *drive out* the demons [italics mine]" (28:18-19). Now, who are the dead if not the Christians who look to us for direction? How can we refuse to respond or vacillate, using the excuse that we neither know the Gospel nor how to communicate it powerfully? Who are the lepers if not those afflicted with myriads of moral choices and medical needs?

Just as in the Old Testament leprosy separated a person from God, so the leprosy of moral confusion and indecision separates us from experiencing the freedom and fullness of Christ. Who are the demons if not the secular ideologies of this age, who pull and tug at all Christians alike to subscribe to their spiritually unbalanced and unrefined world views. They urge the afflicted Christian to act according to his own need and to avoid judging the appropriateness of his behavior in terms of Christ's revealed message to us. Although the Church realizes that this great commission is often neglected by clergy and laity alike, it nevertheless always admonishes as Paul did Timothy: "Devote yourself to the public reading of

Scripture . . . be diligent in these matters and give yourself completely to them; watch your life and doctrine closely" (1 Timothy 4:13).

Second, regarding the idea that the basis for our response should come from our Orthodox confession of Faith: We have already seen that as a royal priesthood—a holy nation—we are commissioned to respond to the scientific and technological advances surrounding us. The fulcrum here is whether we choose to respond to these issues in a disciplined and skillful manner, using Christ as our model, His message as our content, and the Holy Spirit as the source of our insight.

Whether we will use the myriad of humanistic and anthropocentric approaches of various competing psychologies to human nature or the many medical theories concerning appropriate responses to human illness, these disciplines, unlike our first choice, do not contain within themselves the power to save a person from the crushing weight of his dilemma but can only address, if anything, his temporal symptoms.

The eminent Episcopal theologian, Morton Kelsey, recently completed a study of the resources used for healing mankind's hurts. He studied them comparatively, examining the references in textbooks available to practitioners of the healing arts in the nineteenth century and comparing them to references in twentieth century textbooks. He specifically looked for references to Scripture and classical Patristic texts bearing on health-care issues: St. John Chrysostom's *On the Priesthood*, St. Augustine's *Confessions*, St. Gregory the Great's *Pastoral Rule*, and St. Cyprian's *Epistles to the Churches*, to name only a few. The startling but not unpredictable conclusion emerged that, whereas the earlier textbooks made frequent use of Scripture and Patristics to assist in moral choices having to do with health and technology related issues, the later texts not only omitted any reference whatsoever to Scripture or Tradition, but also presented a series of psycho-social and medical theories—each judged on equal footing with the other—as the primary options for evaluating the appropriateness of health-care intervention. As the century progresses, it would appear, we have built in the bias of looking exclusively to the secular sciences for informed insight into moral problems. What has become of the "great commission"? The presuppositions of the spirit of the times has rewritten it so as to exchange the revealed and holistic truth about man as expressed by Christ in the Old and New Testaments and applied historically over time by those most familiar with the compartmentalized views of human nature as they are often disparately stated in the various behavioral and medical subspecialties. We have slowly but surely exchanged the eternal Truth about the goal of human nature—to be "partakers of the Divine Nature" (2 Peter 1:4) and the goal of salvation to be the ultimate purpose of problem-solving—for the ever-changing and historically relative truths about the antecedents of human behavior as originating in real-life or laboratory environments.

I hasten to add that I am not saying that the conclusions of the natural and behavioral sciences are irrelevant to us in forming our Christian response to the solution of human problems. There is no *prima facie* polarity between a Scriptural and Traditional approach and a scientific approach to problem-solving. We must always remind ourselves that God's revealed Truth continues in the natural world and in the natural sciences just as it does in the sacred sciences. However, the issue is one of balance and of the criteria employed for the evaluation of discovery. We must seek balance through evaluation and synthesis, where possible, between the orientation, content, and findings of the natural and applied sciences and the eternal revelation of the Gospel, the image of man that it presents, and the ministry of Jesus as a model for human response as recorded in the various scriptures.

Perhaps the best summary of the effect of over-weighting natural science's response to the human condition is given by St. Gregory the Great in his *Pastoral Rule*: "There is nothing remarkable in wishing to make man the image and likeness of the universe. Thinking to elevate man, these people do not notice they give him the same characteristics of the mosquito or mouse. Yet, it is perfection that distinguishes him from the created and changeable order." Echoing the same sentiment, St. John Chrysostom writes: "There is but one method and way of healing after we have gone wrong and that is the powerful application of the Word" (*On the Priesthood*).

The model that I wish to present as a prototypical Christian response to the moral dimension of human problems stems from the above two writers: 1) it is a model based upon the church's doctrine of personhood; 2) it is a model that uses the tools of Scripture and Tradition to enlighten, evaluate, and interact with the procedures and discoveries of the natural and human sciences as they impact the moral dimension of reality; and 3) it is a model that takes into account the triadic relationship between practitioner, patient, and God Himself at those life-coordinates where decisions—personal or public—must be made.

To sum up at this point: The contributions of the Orthodox understanding of the creation and fall of man illuminates his search for the discovery of the proper code of morality and system of ethics by:

1) Answering the *metaphysical* question: Who am I? Rather than considering ourselves simply as beings with specific social/psychological and demographic profiles, our response is that men and women are creatures meant to be "partakes of the Divine Nature"; that is, to know the good and share in the benefits of following it. Though this ability is no longer an ascribed quality of human nature, it is still attainable by contact with God in His Church.

2) Answering the *ontological* question: Where did I come from? From Scripture we respond that we came from the love of God, who so loved the totality of His creation that he wished to create a being in His own image and likeness with the capacity to discern and act upon the perceived good in the natural order. This love covenant establishes, therefore, a reciprocity of duties

and obligations in response to our God as Creator, and these duties and responsibilities are outlined and evaluated by the study of his word—his intention—for us.

3)   Answering the *teleological* question: What is my destiny? Our destiny is salvation, and this answer emphasizes the importance of examining each and every one of our acts in terms of its contributing to or diminishing the attainment of this goal.

These posed and answered metaphysical, ontological and teleological questions complement and expand the nature of man beyond what has been discovered in the natural sciences. In answer to metaphysical question, the natural and social sciences may well answer that a man is a collection of his feelings, attitudes, and perceptions about himself and others. In answering the ontological question, these sciences may respond from a hereditary or environmentalist point of view. In answering the teleological question, these disciplines may well focus on solutions to various life problems. To all these responses, we Orthodox assent, but we also assert that men and women are all of these but also "these plus." And this "plus" is the flame of the Divine in human nature that searches for the good and the right but recognizes its source—though a personal one—as outside of itself, in Incarnate God Himself, who is willing to cooperate with this search and enter into personal human histories in order to attain the goal of the good, of the right. Such is the legacy of the Saints.

It is at this this coordinate of the search for the good and the right and the entrance into personal human histories of Almighty God Himself that our Christian response to the natural multiplicity of human moral options comes face-to-face with the *kerygma* of and concerning Christ—not only the proclamation of His atoning "works," but also the explication of their meaning. And it is within this kerygma as taught by the Church that we receive the discernment not only to search for the good and the right, but also to seek to understand it when it is found and apply it to our lives when it is needed. This kerygma is encapsulated in St. Paul's statement that ". . . the gospel . . . it is the power of God for the salvation of everyone" (Romans 1:16). Using the word *power*, St. Paul emphasizes that it is every Christian's task to facilitate moral decision-making in himself or in others by bringing a real, heart-felt experience of salvation to bear on a defined human need.

What model, then, emerges from the kerygma of Scripture that can serve as a salvation-based solution to our moral dilemmas as well as provide the content for responding, witnessing, and modelling the right and the good in our behavior? The components of this model are as follows:

1)   We recall a word or activity of Christ and apply it to our natural situations. In other words, we observe our human action under the enlightenment of God's word and tradition.

2)   We recognize the unity of a person's mind, body, and soul and minister to

each so as to bring about a contact point between the person and the Grace of God. Our starting point is Jesus Christ, and from that vantage point we teach about human nature and the human situation. We approach this task from His graciousness, and we are both admonished and guided by His interpretation of our situation.

3) We make a deliberate attempt to apply a consistent understanding of the kerygma to ourselves and to people in need.

4) We recognize that authentic and holistic existence comes to us as a gift of Grace, mediated once and for all through Christ, who is eternally present in the world through His Church—the repository of His teaching and direction.

5) We understand that God makes Himself known through the Incarnation and that through His ministry and life certain expectations about our personhood and its options for change and development are made known.

6) We make Faith an active part of our love of and learning about Jesus.

7) We show that a Christian witness is a witness to the Truth by studying an applying God's revelation. We are, thereby, able to understand ourselves and others.

8) We realize that the reality of God is also taught by our own examples.

9) We realize that the discernment of the proper direction to take in life crises can only be brought about by faith and grace, and we never assume that we have either but seek to understand the word of God, thereby, receiving each.

10) We interpret Christ's actions as giving explicit meaning to all human events.

11) We communicate the "Good News" of Christ as precisely that point in our own and others' lives where need evidences itself.

12) We realized that the authentic proclamation of the kerygma involves not just words but a demonstration of the power of God's love as it applies in concrete circumstances.

13) We realize that our abilities to choose rest not in ourselves but derive from Christ as the source of all healing—the *therapon* for the sick and broken.

14) We realize that this Christian response and guidance is a sign of God's reconciling power in the world.

As our model, Christ used methods of response that were guided by their congruence to the will of the Father and the nature of the moral dilemma itself. We, too, must adopt these modes as ways to put into operation the kerygma. As

St. Paul instructs Timothy: "The sins of some men are obvious . . . the sins of others trail behind them" (Timothy 5:24). With the woman caught in adultery, he uses compassion; with the know-it-all teachers, he uses confrontation. With others, still, he teaches the importance of support and sensitivity. But in each case, he teaches us the importance of listening closely to another person in order to discern both the problem and the solution and, after our discernment, to skillfully design and guide our inquiry so that our hearers feel the power of God in their lives and can sharpen their spiritual eye of discernment in the midst of moral problems, options, and competing ideologies. And, finally, Christ as our model was spiritually mature, evidencing the necessity of the knowledge of Scripture: "For all Scripture is inspired and God-breathed and useful for teaching, rebuking, correcting and training" (2 Timothy 3:16).

We are now at the very threshold of understanding how to implement these tools of the kerygma of Scripture to discern right from wrong options, to guide moral decision-making, and to supplement and direct our professional efforts. The Apostles, the Fathers, and we as mediators of the kerygma and imitators of Christ accomplish these things by nurturing the Holy Spirit within us and in those who come to us for help. It is the Holy Spirit, we are taught, who "searches all things, who knows the thoughts of God," and who allows us to share in what God has freely given us in the ministry of Jesus (1 Corinthians 1:10-12). The Holy Spirit imparts to us the love for God (Romans 15:13), teaches us how to act (John 14:26), reproves (John 16:8), helps our infirmities (Romans 8:26), testifies to the reality of Christ in our lives (John 15:16), and "leads us into all truth." These gifts of the Holy Spirit are the very practical goals of Christian decision-making. As St. Gregory of Nyssa writes: "The grace of God is not able to visit those who flee salvation. Nor is human virtue of such power as to be adequate of itself to raise up to authentic life, those souls untouched by Grace. But when righteousness of works [man's action] and the Grace of the Holy Spirit [God action] come together at the same time in the same soul, together they are able to endow it with a blessed life." And what is a blessed life if not a good life, a right life, a full life?

Understanding, then, that our tasks are to appropriate, act upon, and model the solutions to our moral dilemmas in light of our salvation, we see how a Christian response bedrocked in the kerygma differs intrinsically from a purely secular model of response. The realm of the secular is by definition always *diadic:* a relationship exist only between the caregiver and patient and is defined in terms of the expressed need of the patient and the insight of the care giver. The process of problem-solving is two-way: The patient expresses his needs, wants and desires, satisfactions and dissatisfactions, and the practitioner evaluates and organizes them, trying to arrange them into a more efficient pattern. However, the Christian response to moral choice is always *triadic.* Not only is there the relationship between patient and practitioner, but standing invisibly above each and acting as both the guide and response for problem-solving is God Himself, who in the process of decision-making provides the kerygma as the ground in which to discover the answers to the patient's questions and the standards by which to evaluate their feasibility as salvational solutions.

I have purposely left until now the fleshing out of the second aim of our Christocentric frame of reference: the notion that if we as Christians do not develop a coherent response to moral problems, the world will. It will accomplish this response by means of its secular understanding of man, his place in the universe, and the goal of his existence and according to the cognitive structures uninformed by Divine and Revealed Truth. In fact, these categories are often so incongruous with kerygma that they appear, from the Christian vantage point, as a ghastly charade of the Divine Plan.

As an example, I will recount what happened on a program recently aired nationally on the *Radio Show*. The subject of the program was the feasibility of terminating life before a fetus comes to term.

The discussant was Dr. Richard Paulsen of the University of Southern California Medical School, who presented theories and fielded questions concerning the beginning of human life. His appearance was prompted by recent litigations involving the custody and viability of in vitro fertilized eggs after the marriage in which they were conceived was dissolved.

To resume our linguistic analogy: If the grammar of the theme of this paper provides insights into the nature and solutions of solving moral problems, the content of this interview provides the syntax—the environment in which our vocabulary functions and with which it both confronts and gains meaning. This syntax is itself informative in the scope of the paper.

Early on in the abortion controversy, neologisms were used rampantly in an effort to avoid the Scriptural and Patristic truth that confesses that life begins at conception. Instead of the familiar chronology of sperm meeting egg and producing a human being, finer distinctions were made: "pre-embryos," "embryos," "conceptii." In place of human life emerging from the union of sperm and egg, a neutral category of "human tissue" has resulted. By some magic of suspending the rules of logical inclusiveness, "human tissue" might be disposed of—no longer a "human being." Complex discussions of when cell development results in the change from human tissue to human nature replaced what used to be a relatively simple chronology of prenatal development.

But perhaps even more indicative than the above of the hurdles involved in a spiritually unbalanced, "medical technology-only" approach to reproduction were the criteria used for making choices about "pregnancy termination." When asked by both the sympathetic interviewer, who shared the reasonableness of this open-minded system, or questioned by at-time hostile guest as to guidelines that could *standardize* decision-making about when human life or human tissue is terminate; not once was any theology of human creation invoked. The Church—any church—was apparently deemed unworthy to offer any sensible guidelines in this scientific wonderland of distinctions heaped on distinctions. Rather, it was concluded that the factors in birthing a child would be discussed in consultation between the medical and legal professions. When implored for an answer to who or what would provide guidelines as to the legitimacy of in vitro fertilization in different circumstances, the audience was comforted with the thought that such guidelines would soon be forthcoming from the American Fertilization Society. No doubt, a comfort to the Christian, indeed!

When at last importuned by interviewer and audience alike that eventually issues of pregnancy termination and "human tissue custody" must boil down to some concept of the beginnings of life, the response—to borrow a metaphor from Lewis Carroll—"the mountain growned and gave forth a molehill." "Well," responded Dr. Paulsen, "I really don't know.—I'd hate to pull things out of bibles." And regarding the potential science of cloning: "Well, there's something wrong with that. We are meant to be born and to die".

I maintain that one does not need a degree in dogmatic theology to see there is something profoundly wrong and gloriously incomplete in this medical world view with its technological outcomes. As representative of the technologies that are emerging that are uninformed by any theological insight into the nature of man, his creation, and destiny, these systems of scientific knowledge are neither the humane solution to the human problems they attest to be, nor are they even faithful to their charter to "relieve human misery and suffering." And the reason is simple: By the admission of their own practitioners, these disciplines provide within themselves no adequate answer to guide or limit their use. They depend upon external systems to delimit their usage—even if this external system is as diffuse and confused as the "bibles" mentioned in the above interview. The simultaneous denial of any external system to inform the technological procedure or its human operator is assumed to be axiomatic. Left to itself, the logical outcome can only be chaos in application and anarchy in its potential. When these two conditions occur we can be certain as Christians that the Lord's will and design is not present, and that it is our duty, not our option, to rise up against them. As is written in Isaiah: "For thus says the Lord . . . who did not create it [the world] in waste . . . I did not say to seed of Jacob 'seek me in chaos'" (45:18-19).

Moral choices grounded in personal expediency are not necessarily lawful, to borrow from the Apostle Paul. The most frightening of them bear certain orientations in common, of which we as Christians need to be aware so that we may not only oppose them but through identifying their common denominators, locate their practitioners that are the most in need of confrontation with the kerygma of Christ. These orientations:

1) Are concerned greatly with expediency, which is the method of problem solving that results from a denial of the Divine in man or man in the Divine; hence, it repudiates of the creation of man in God's image and the Incarnation of Christ as the means of appropriating saving grace;

2)   Can be identified as propagating false ideas about God and man's relations to Him;

3)   May also he ignorant of God and His promises or have an absence of faith in Him or His word.

When these conditions are present in a discipline or an orientation, the boundary of moral option has been passed over and, through technological procedure, sin has been put into operation as a conscious and willful rebellion against God and His saving works.

We are at last in a position to understand the etiology and component parts of our fourth and final aim: the integral and integrative principle of our personal Christian experience as the basis to respond to, prioritize, and operationalize the new technologies based on developing medical knowledge and new, emergent human conditions of suffering. Our thrust now must change from "Physician heal thy patient" to "Physician heal thyself." We as health practitioners must develop the same Christocentric focus and continuity in our responses to circumstances within our own physical reality that we expect to elicit and put into operation in the lives of others.

Our integration arises from recognizing our spiritual vocation as being the guiding principle for our professional avocation. Initiated by baptism, nurtured by the grace of the sacraments, this vocation is nothing less than *theosis*. Theosis is the process of bringing body and spirit in conformity with the revealed will of God as discovered in his unique plan for us. It is a process of an interior reaching out towards God and an exterior monitoring and evaluating all of our behavioral and professional responses in light of the kerygma of Christ. We keep as our goal our Lord's command to "be perfect, as you Father in heaven is perfect" in each and every circumstance and diverse happening of life (Matthew 5:48). We have as a means of attaining this goal the acquisition of the Incarnate Christ by faith through cultivating the Holy Spirit's charisms, which have been freely given us. It was St. Paul's wish that ". . . Christ may dwell in your hearts through faith and you may comprehend the width, the length, the depth, the height of all things . . . that you may be filled with the fullness of God"—in other words, that we may not only have knowledge of all things but realize Christ's presence in all things (Ephesians 3: 14-19).

If in our personal lives we recognize and honor the centrality of the Divine self-disclosure as our guiding principle, but in our work-a-day lives if we exchange the fundamental truths discovered in Scripture, Tradition, and Holy Spirit insight for the derivative and partial truths of our professional disciplines, we will find ourselves bifurcated—split-personality Christians. Christians we are, but only partially so. We will be unable to provide coherent responses to the moral dilemmas of our times either within our own lives or as Christocentric witnesses to others. While grounding our own lives in the truth of God's word in Christ, our piety will remain personal—unobservable and unreplicable. When called upon to exercise our charism of discernment in our role as care-givers to others, we will feel woefully inadequate in the certainty of our moral decisions, and rather than a journey towards Truth, our Christian walk will become an uncomfortable accommodation of making the least wrong decisions.

We all read textbook upon textbook and attend symposium heaped on symposium, seeking to learn more about the pharmacology, symptomatology, and phenomenolgy of the physical, psychological, and sociological ills endemic in us and in our society. When confronted with human need in our professional capacities, we put the same God we worship and adore in our liturgical and spiritual life on the shelf, and run to the latest secular scientific discovery to guide our attempts to help individuals solve their problems and meet their need. If, therefore, we as Christians find ourselves moderately successful in our caregiving task but internally disquieted by the uncertainty of the correlation between solution and salvation, it is because we to borrow our Savior's metaphor, are ourselves a house divided. We do not sufficiently realize the full meaning and implication of our Lord's statement, "The kingdom of God is within you," and we fail to realize that we will never be able to read all the available scientific texts bearing upon solving the problems of the human condition. In short, we do not fully realize that we do not even have to undertake this exhausting task most of the times. Rather, all that is necessary is the one thing that is needful: to carry over into our professional lives our identity as adopted sons of God, made personal by faith in Christ—our identity as Christians, in short—and to generalize the means and methods for discerning the good, the right, and the true we develop and practice in our personal spiritual lives into the public performance of our professions.

Part Two

Genetic Engineering: Where Do We Draw the Line?

The Challenge of Genetic Research

Peter H. Diamandis

Man's reach has extended to the outer limits of the universe; he has probed into the inner confines of the atomic nucleus and has altered the molecular basis of life itself. Time and time again barriers that were once thought sacred have toppled and regions of thought known only to God have become incorporated into man's amassed knowledge. Today, as molecular biologists contemplate improving on life, astronomers theorize about the origins of the universe, and scientists plan to transplant human life onto other worlds, people are beginning to raise serious questions about these activities. What right does man have to move in these directions? Was he meant to have the key to the most basic essence of God's creations? Does the exploration into the mystery of the universe comply with God's plan? Should governments spend exorbitant funds and time on this type of research when thousands die each day from hunger and exposure?

Without doubt the field of research that most challenges our ethical and religious values is genetic engineering. Today, molecular biologists have unraveled a significant portion of the DNA genetic code—the instruction set that directs growth, metabolism, and reproduction in every cell of the body. Work in genetics has progressed to the point where scientists can actually consider improving upon what already exists—what God has created. Though pretentious, it may soon be within man's ability to produce larger farm animals that would provide more meat, larger eggs, or more milk. It is also conceivable that families that carry a trait for a particular genetic disease may be able to have their genes corrected. Thus thalasemics, or sickle cell carriers, could bare children without the fear of passing on the disease.

43

In the near future, the term "designer jeans (genes)" may take on new meaning as parents preselect what their children should look and act like: what gender, how tall, what color, how smart. Is it heresy to think that man has the right to consider such moves? Where would he stop? Surely being able to correct genetic disease is both moral and ethical, but once scientists can control a few genetic outcomes, would not parents want their children to be taller, more muscular, more intelligent, with hair and eye color of their choice?

In this presentation, I hope first to give an historical background to demonstrate how rapidly our understanding of genetics has been developing. I hope also to present a simplified overview of what genetic engineering encompasses, of what exists as the current state of the art, of the almost completed plans for treating disease in humans, and finally a glimpse at what this revolutionary technology might give us in the next few decades. Primarily, I would like to point out many of the dilemmas that genetic engineering might create for us in the near and not-to-distant future.

HISTORICAL PERSPECTIVE

The science of genetics—the understanding that a living creature's appearance is controlled by inherited instructions called genes—was established in 1865 by a modest Austrian monk named Gregor Mendel. Unfortunately, as with most significant breakthroughs, Mendel's ideas were not initially accepted. It was not until the early to mid-twentieth century that our rudimentary understanding of genetics began to progress. Limited by their inability to peer into the microscopic world of the cell's nucleus, scientists were forced to try to understand genetics through crude animal breeding experiments, in which mutations and characteristics such as height and color were followed from generation to generation. It was not until 1953 that scientists finally understood what, in fact, the gene was composed of. In this year Drs. Watson and Crick discovered the structure of DNA (deoxyribonucleic acid), the very "stuff of life."

Even though scientists have known about DNA for over thirty years, genetic engineering—the ability to move genes around, to cut them out of one piece of DNA and stick them into "another"—did not develop until this last decade. Only recently have scientists developed the tools and the understanding to find the location of one gene amongst the fifty thousand found in the body. Likewise, the ability to isolate the gene, cut it out, read it like the words of a book, change it to fit the specific needs, and insert it back to the chosen cells has grown remarkably in less than ten years. Thus we can see that genetic engineering is perhaps the most recent, as well as one of the most powerful, of modern-day technologies.

BASIC THEORY OF GENETIC ENGINEERING

The human body is made up of cells, billions and billions of them. Each of these cells takes on special functions—some of them carry oxygen, some fight infection, some contract, and some conduct electrical signals. Regardless of their specialized function, they all stem from a very basic design from that one cell formed during conception as the female egg became fertilized. The shape that each individual has, the information that determined the structure of each cell in his or her body, is packed into the nucleus of each cell in the body.

To give a basic understanding of genetic engineering, let me first briefly review the basic components of the cell:

Cell: The cell is the basic unit of life. It is able to reproduce (in most cases) and to perform such functions as respiration (energy production), growth, and internal repair. Cells that have similar functions are collectively known as tissues (for example, bone tissue, brain tissue, epidermal tissue, and so forth).

Nucleus: A nucleus is present within every human cell. The nucleus is a membrane-bounded area that contains the genetic material. It also contains the machinery needed for replicating and reading the DNA.

Chromosomes: Chromosomes are the condensed version of the genetic material. They are composed of one long stretch of DNA that folds upon itself many times over. Humans possess two sets of 23 chromosomes one set of which is the sex chromosome. Some genetic diseases, such as Downs Syndrome, can be detected on this level.

DNA: Deoxyribonucleic acid (DNA) is a continuous chain that contains the genetic information. It is made up of four subunits in a manner analogous to a language that has four letters arranged to form words and sentences that the cell can interpret as instructions.

Genes: Genes are the basic units of instruction. In the above analogy, the genes are like sentences. The cell contains over fifty thousand genes. Each gene contains instructions for a particular function. Some genes control when other genes should be read, some contain instructions for the cell to build a protein, and others sense conditions in the environment that indicate whether it is time to divide or to remain dormant.

Nucleotides: Nucleotides comprise the basic letters in the DNA language. There are four different nucleotides, symbolically represented by the letters T, A, C, and G. The order of these nucleotides is crucial for the instruction in the genes to be properly understood. A change in this order (for example, TACGTG → TACATG) due to radiation or chemical mutagens could potentially lead to serious problems.

Proteins: Proteins are the basic workers of the cell. They are coded for, like everything else, by the genes. Some proteins serve as structural supports like beams in a house. Some proteins contract (for example, the muscles); some proteins recognize other molecules in the cell and thus serve as "protein eyes"; some proteins function to cut and splice other molecules (scissors and glue).

Enzymes: Enzymes are those proteins that recognize a particular molecule and split it at a particular point or, conversely, recognize two separate molecules and bring them together in a very specific manner (the scissors and glue mentioned above).

Mutations: Mutations are changes in the nucleotide sequence that result in abnormal genes and, in the final consequence, abnormal proteins and cell functioning.

Inheritable Genetic Disease: This type of disease is caused by a mutation that is passed on from parent to child. In the case of sickle cell anemia the mutation is an inappropriate nucleotide in the gene that codes for the protein hemoglobin.

Conventional medicine treats genetic disease by treating the symptom, rarely the cause—that is, the aberrant protein. The reason for this is simply that, for the most part, such direct treatment is beyond the physician's ability and/or means. Thus diabetes is managed by supplying insulin, not by replacing the genes responsible for the inadequate productions. Imagine, however, if it were possible to enter into each cell of the body that produced the abnormal protein, locate the mutated gene, cut it out, and paste in its place the correct version. The result would be a total cure—not some temporary palliative treatment but a permanent conversion to normalcy. Beyond this, if it were then possible to correct the genes in the germ line cells that give rise to the sperm and ova, then future generations would also be free of disease. The removal of all genetic disease is one of the dreams put forth by genetic engineers.

TODAY'S CUTTING EDGE TECHNOLOGY

The genetic engineering and biotechnologies of today are progressing rapidly, turning the fiction of the last few decades into reality. Without going into detail, a few of the most dramatic developments bear mentioning.

Genetic engineered drugs have recently entered into the marketplace. Produced by bacteria or yeast, pharmaceutical companies are developing new advanced antibiotics; cheaper, purer forms of insulin; and cleaner immunizations against hepatitis.

As physicians and geneticists have started to understand the genetic basis for disease, it has become increasingly possible to perform simple tests to *predict* whether an individual is inflicted by or is a carrier of a particular disease. The tests performed are painless; the researcher needs the DNA from only a few cells.

Such tests seem helpful — after all, this information could be of critical importance to genetic counselors in advising couples who have family histories of a particular disease. However, when closely examined, some ethical questions arise: What if a genetic abnormality is discovered in an individual who is in utero? What if the disease is one that comes in later life, such as Huntington's Chorea? A genetic test showing a positive result early in that individual's life might destroy any hope of his or her leading a normal existence until the time when the disease becomes apparent.

Today, the ability of certain technicians to perform micro-manipulation of subcellular structures is truly phenomenal. Over the years it has become possible not only to isolate an ovulated egg, but also to inject genetic materials into its nucleus. What this research all comes down to is two very impressive capabilities: *in vitro fertilization* and *cloning*.

In vitro fertilization, as most people know, is a reality. It has successfully been performed numerous times. It is, however, still in its primitive state of development. In the future, it is probable that the genetic information used for the fertilization is very carefully selected by the explicit directions of the parents rather than the random union of any sperm and egg.

Cloning is the ability to take one cell from an individual and from it reconstruct the entire person. This technology has existed for years with certain lab animals, such as frogs, mice, and horses, and unsubstantiated rumors tell of two successful cases with humans. Nevertheless, even if the rumors are false, the technology to accomplish cloning in humans is not far off. Science fiction has recounted for years how human clones could be raised for the sole purpose of providing organ transplants. When one's heart, liver, or kidney begins to fail, his or her clone will be ready to provide a perfectly compatible replacement. But is this type of cloning moral? After all, the cell that started the whole clone off belongs to that individual. Another question arises: Does the clone have a soul?

The total genomic content of humans is huge. Human beings have over 50,000 genes that direct their development, metabolism and reproduction. Each human being has trillions of nucleotides, the basic building blocks that make up the letters of the genetic code. Scientists have only deciphered about one percent of these trillions of letters that describe man in detail. Over the past two to three years, scientists' ability to "sequence genomic DNA" — in other words, to read these letters, has increased immensely. It was recently suggested that an intensive effort to completely read and record the entire genetic code of humans be undertaken. Such a project would require hundreds of man-years and billions of dollars and would essentially produce an encyclopedia filled with a four-letter alphabet describing man's make-up in the most basic detail.

What are the religious implications of such an event? Man would be reduced to an extensive description, a series of letters, a complicated instruction booklet.

Molecular technology not only allows biologists to read a DNA sequence, but also to create one. Biologists have successfully strung together nucleotides that create stretches of DNA. Is it then possible that a geneticist—given enough time and with the proper equipment, as well as the Encyclopedia of the human genetic code— could create a human being from commonly available chemicals. Obviously, the issue is much more complex than slapping together the proper molecules, but this possibility begins to raise fundamental questions about the essential nature of man: Is the human begin more than a very complicated assemblage of the proper atoms? What and where is the spirit or the soul? As man begins to better understand the human body at the most basic levels, such questions begin to weigh very heavily.

Perhaps one of the most graphic presentations of genetic engineering was the insertion of an additional growth hormone gene into a line of lab mice. This new breed of "super-mice" was approximately twice the size of the original breed. Such experiments represent only the beginning of scientists' abilities to enhance or diminish certain characteristics of living organisms. Such manipulations may result in live-stock that are larger, healthier, and tastier.

The final, and perhaps most important consideration of today's cutting edge technology is in the area that has been termed "gene-therapy." In simple terms, gene therapy is the process of providing a patient with a normal copy of the gene he or she does not possess. In practice, a patient with a particular genetic disease—for example, sickle cell anemia—would receive an injection of highly modified viruses that would seek out specific cells in the body and infect them. In the case of sickle cell anemia, the virus would seek out the bone marrow stem cells that are the precursors to the hemoglobin-producing cell. After infecting those cells, the viruses would insert their DNA into the nucleus as many viruses normally do. The beauty of this system lies in the fact that the viruses were initially modified to remove the pathogenic genes of the virus and replace them with the gene of choice—in this case, the normal hemoglobin gene. Thus, the virus has, in essence, functioned as a messenger to identify the proper cells and deliver to them the particular gene of interest. Today, this technique, though promising, still has a number of unsolved problems, such as the regulation of the genes once inserted into the genome.

LOOKING INTO THE FUTURE

As fantastic as genetic engineering seems and as disturbing as some of its possibilities appear, it is only the rudimentary manifestation of a much more complex and powerful technology known as molecular engineering, or nanotechnology. Molecular engineering is a field whose implications are just now beginning to be grasped. The technology is one that manipulates objects at the molecular and atomic levels—thus the prefix *nano* (nanotechnology). One can hardly imagine what might be possible if the capability to control the assembly of structures on such a fine level is within man's reach.

Scientists in the field of molecular engineering are today working on molecular computers that are perhaps as powerful as personal computers but are so small that they fit into the average human cell and take up only one hundredth (1/100) of the volume. In addition to these nanocomputers, theorists are contemplating the construction of nanomachinery—molecular-sized machinery that has the capability to recognize certain atoms or molecules, pick them up, move them about, and attach them to other building blocks. Such nanomachines are not inconceivable. In his book *Engines of Creation*, K. Eric Drexler, a research affiliate of the MIT Space Systems Laboratory, points out that ribosomes, enzymes, bacterial flagellas, ion pumps, and a variety of natural subcellular structures are really nanomachines. Drexler demonstrates how this technology can be used to assemble molecules atom by atom, in any combination of interest, thus producing nearly every conceivable substance or device within the limits of nature. Such a technology will surely revolutionize healing.

Medicine has been, and is today, a very gross and inexacting technology. Doctors deal with some diseased organs by cutting them out, and with cancers by baking them with radiation; they treat diseases with chemicals that have broad and often unknown interactions. Doctors treat their patients with these methods because that is the best that they can do. Healing in its ultimate form is not just palliative but instead the act of returning the body—each and every cell—to its perfect state of being. Imagine for a moment what would happen if doctors were in fact able to do this—to remove the accumulated waste and repair the protein cross-linking damage caused by aging in every cell of the body. The result is summarized in one word—immortality. When asked about the prospect of molecular technology, Dr. Gene Brown, professor of biochemistry at MIT, said, "Given sufficient time and effort to develop artificial molecular machines and to conduct detailed studies of the molecular biology of the cell, very broad abilities should emerge. Among these could be the ability to separate the proteins in cross-linked structures, and to identify, repair, and replace them."

Genetic engineering and molecular engineering will give humanity unbelievable capabilities. But, as with any technology since the advent of fire, the ability to accomplish the greatest good parallels the ability to do the greatest harm.

In the future, this technology *will* without doubt give us life-saving drugs, cure some genetic diseases, and give us a better scientific understanding of the make up of the human being. In the future, this technology *may* lead to immortality and new life forms, but perhaps, on the negative side, to germ warfare and abominations of the human form. In the future, we must learn where to draw the line in genetic engineering. Genetic and molecular engineering may in fact not have any limitations other than those imposed on them by the laws of nature.

For the present, what is needed most is educated individuals—people who do not blindly demand a stop to this research, but people who provide informed guidance, feedback, and support to the researchers and overseeing institutions that exist today. It is in this role that I hope religious institutions will become involved.

Genetic Engineering: Setting the Limits

John Breck

The very expression *genetic engineering* has an ominous ring to it. It suggest manipulation and, consequently, violation of human life at its most basic level. At worst, it conjures up images of newly created life forms, whereby a select few will achieve the status of Nietzschean "supermen," while others are reduced to humanoids that will constitute an inferior servant class.

In any discussion of the ethics of genetic engineering, it is important to separate fact from myth and possibility from fantasy. Genetic engineering holds out extraordinary hope for improving the quality of human life by increasing the quality and abundance of crops and livestock; by producing insulin, interferon, hormones, vaccines, and so forth for use by humans; and by making available products that would improve the environment, such as enzymes to break down industrial wastes, fertilizers developed from nitrogen rather than from oil, and inexpensive, relatively pollution-free automotive fuels.

Yet, like many products of modern technology, genetic engineering is inherently dangerous. If it promises to correct genetic anomalies, improve intelligence, and provide offspring to infertile couples, it could serve as well—presumably in the near future—to produce genetic hybrids, a master race, or the ultimate weapon for use in germ warfare. The question "Where do we draw the limits?" is therefore an urgent one that the Church must raise *now* and to which she must give a clear and firm answer. Such an answer must somehow guarantee both legal enforcement and continual ethical review. In this brief paper I can only state the nature of the

51

problem and attempt to indicate how such limits should be determined.

We should begin with a few basic definitions. The science of *genetics*, which came into its own at the beginning of this century with the rediscovery of Gregor Mendel's laws of heredity, is the branch of biology that studies the genes or units of the chromosome that transmit specific traits and genetic defects. Between 50,000 and 100,000 genes are located on each of the forty-six chromosomes contained within the nucleus of every human cell. Often referred to as the blueprints of our heredity, genes are composed of segments of deoxyribonucleic acid (DNA), which in turn comprise four chemical subunits that determine the genetic code of inherited characteristics.

The science of *eugenics* investigates, develops, and applies methods for improving the genetic code of particular individuals and of the human gene pool as a whole. A distinction is usually made between negative and positive eugenics. Negative eugenics refers to various forms of intervention that seek to eliminate genetic defects. It begins with genetic screening to discover defective genes within the parent that might be transmitted to the child; or, by the process of amniocentesis, it seeks to discover whether the fetus is afflicted with abnormalities such as Downs syndrome, the XYY syndrome, hemophilia, spina bifida, or cystic fibrosis. Genetic counseling based upon that screening then recommends an appropriate course of action: contraception, abortion of the fetus, or, where possible, "genetic surgery" to correct the problem *in utero*. Negative eugenics, then, aims essentially at prevention and therapy.

Positive eugenics, on the other hand, strives to improve what are understood to be normal and desirable traits, with the purpose of creating a superior human being. A fundamental moral problem arises here with the determination of the criteria of excellence: Who decides, and on what grounds, which traits are in fact the most desirable? In our production/consumption-oriented society, where economic forces prevail and competition is exalted as a supreme virtue, traits such as intelligence, ingenuity, and aggressiveness would surely be valued above the human qualities Jesus identified in the Beatitudes (Matthew 5) or St. Paul included in his list of the "fruit of the Spirit" (Gal. 5). Positive eugenics raises other ethical problems as well, in that its methods and goals would encourage widespread use of in vitro fertilization, embryo transplants into surrogate mothers and artificial insemination that uses the sperm of an anonymous donor rather than that of the husband.

Because both negative and positive eugenics can in principle employ some of the same methods to achieve their aims (for example, in vitro fertilization, recombinant DNA techniques, or "gene splicing"), it would seem more appropriate to label them respectively *therapeutic* and *innovational* eugenics. For, ironically, an Orthodox moral perspective would judge negative eugenics as potentially capable of attaining positive and desirable therapeutic results, whereas so called "positive" eugenics would have to be rejected as unwarranted tampering with human life created in the image and likeness of God. While Christian people can and ought to support research into the area of therapeutic eugenics, they cannot morally condone other forms of research in which the basic principle of self-determination is violated by techniques of manipulation.

Does genetic engineering, then, constitute therapeutic or innovational eugenics? The concept of eugenics, like the concept of euthanasia, tends to promise more than it can deliver. Insofar as the acceptance of euthanasia can lead to "death on demand" through the willful taking of human life by suicide or authorized murder, it violates the very principle of a good death. In fact, given the tragic nature of death as both a cause and a consequence of human sin, it is questionable whether the expression *good death* has any meaning at all or whether it is merely a contradiction in terms. However that may be, the Church's prayer is for "a Christian ending to our life." Yet we also pray that that ending be "painless, blameless, and peaceful." Appropriate therapy—using certain drugs, even when they might impair reason and hasten death in terminal patients, and allowing various forms of medical intervention, including withdrawal of life support system—is, therefore, acceptable and is, in fact, required by an Orthodox approach to bio-ethics to permit the natural dying process to occur with a maximum of consciousness and a minimum of suffering. If properly defined and practiced so as to preserve and enhance the spiritual, mental, and physical well-being of the terminally ill patient, what is called passive euthanasia can be morally acceptable in certain cases.

Therapeutic eugenics is to the beginning of human life what appropriate passive euthanasia is to its physical end. Similarly, innovational eugenics corresponds to active euthanasia and must likewise be condemned. Ethicians are particularly concerned with the risk of narrowing the human gene pool and the consequences of circumventing the natural evolutionary process by employing innovative techniques in the conception and development of human life. Still more serious are the implications that innovational eugenics has for spiritual growth: the interior movement towards the union with divine life that we term *theosis*, or divinization. Such growth is only possible within the fallen created order through a process of continual repentance and the free exercise of moral choice that permits the practice of such virtues as altruism, kindness, generosity, devotion—in a word, Christian love. A growing number of specialists in the fields of eugenics and sociobiology, however, hold that such moral virtues are, in fact, biologically determined—that, like vices such as greed and egotism, they are the direct expression of our individual genetic programs.

For years debates have focused on the relationship between genetic factors and environment in determining human behavior. (For example: "Is intelligence related to race?"; "Are criminality and violence due to an extra Y chromosome?"; and so forth.) Orthodox anthropology rejects *a priori* any "hard determinism" that would reduce a human being to a caricature of itself by denying the person the God-given freedom to make choices, to establish personal relationships, and to exercise the spiritual options of repentance and reconciliation.

What should our criteria be, then, for determining the limits within which genetic engineering may be ethically practiced? And how can we, as Orthodox Christians, gain the leverage in our society, marked as it is by a certain "techno-idolatry" and passion for the new and untried, to ensure that the Orthodox position will be heard, and, where necessary, legally enforced?

Because of the gravity and urgency of the problem posed by the potential misuse of genetic technology, the first step that should be taken is the creation of an inter-Orthodox Ethical Review Committee. Such a committee, selected from among physicians, scientists, and theologians who are familiar with bio-ethical issues, should be given the official approval and blessing of the Standing Conference of Orthodox Bishops in America (S.C.O.B.A.). Furthermore, it should receive adequate funding from our various jurisdictional treasuries to provide research facilities and the secretarial staff needed to monitor and to disseminate information to the Church as well as to the general public. Close cooperation with similar groups within the Roman Catholic and Protestant churches would be indispensable. A multitude of questions arises with such a suggestion: how would the criteria for selecting members, to ensure both competence and the absence of vested interest be determined; how would adequate financing be guaranteed; how would appropriate methods for acquiring and publicizing relevant information be developed, and so on. Good will and informed concern, however, can resolve such problems and remove inevitable obstacles.

The work of such a committee should be complemented by other initiatives: by creating special seminary courses in bio-ethics that are open to a broad spectrum of the public; by including position papers in Church publications and popular journals; and by generally raising the level of consciousness of our Orthodox people to the potential for good as well as to the dangers inherent in genetic research. It would be as morally wrong for us to hinder research and the application of proper therapeutic methods that result from it as it would be to remain silent in the face of evident abuses.

This position means, however, that we as Orthodox must work not only to inform our faithful of new developments—of both promising ventures and risks—in the field of genetic engineering. We must also seek appropriate ways and means to press for *adequate legislation* and other safeguards, both for ourselves and for the public at large.

Finally, we must be willing to engage in an effort of continual review. Technology is developing today at a prodigious rate, especially in areas of genetics and microbiology. Certain techniques already exist that Orthodox Christians simply cannot accept and still remain faithful to the Gospel and Tradition. Such techniques include abortion (with the rarest of exceptions where the life of the mother is truly endangered), forced sterilization to prevent the transmission of undesirable genetic traits, artificial insemination using the sperm of an anonymous donor, in vitro fertilization involving the freezing and storing of embryos, surrogate mothering, and, in general, any technique by which man attempts to recreate man in his own image. Each of these techniques proves inadmissible because each inevitably dehumanizes the person involved. Although in vitro fertilization and artificial insemination using the husband's sperm may in some cases be ethically acceptable, should the Church not rather urge its members to *adopt*, given the masses of eligible children throughout the world? Whereas cloning—the artificial production of an identical twin—holds out tremendous promise for agriculture, must not the Church condemn it as grotesque genetic manipulation when it is practiced on human beings? While the embryo has no discernible level of consciousness and might appear to be an appropriate subject for abortion or genetic experimentation, does not the Church celebrate liturgically the *conception* of her Lord and the saints, thus placing ultimate personal value on the conceptus not only as a viable human person but as a bearer of the divine image?

While these and similar questions must be given firm and unambiguous answers by Christian people and by the Church as a whole, they should not be allowed to blind us to the truly marvellous possibilities that the science of genetic engineering offers us today for the betterment of human life tomorrow. Although genetic engineering is in its infancy, new developments occur so rapidly that continual reassessment of bio-possibilities and bio-hazards is imperative. As with any ethical issue, each particular case must be judged and evaluated on its own merits within its own context. This assertion does not mean, however, that we are bound by a "situational ethic." Orthodox moral theology is based upon absolute truths— upon Him who is the Truth itself—and its judgments can and must be informed and guided by Holy Tradition as well as by the potential inherent in any particular technological achievement.

Orthodox Tradition demands absolute respect for the integrity and freedom of the person. Determining the appropriate limits to genetic engineering, or to any other technique or process that can irreversibly affect human nature itself can only be done appropriately and faithfully in so far as such respect for the person guides our judgements from the moment of life's conception until its fulfillment at death.

Part Three

Depression: A Case Study

Case Presentation

History

The patient is an 80 year-old white male with significant arthritis. His wife, who had been his main support, died thirteen months ago. The patient had been doing well until one month ago, when, on the anniversary of his wife's death, he attempted suicide.

The patient now lives alone in a trailer. He has a daughter who helps him but has other responsibilities as well. The patient states that he does not want to be dependent on his daughter. The patient also states that he is disgusted with himself. He does not think he will ever get well but will always be a "cripple."

Physical

The patient appears to be an elderly white male, in a wheelchair, who is alert and responsive. He appears mildly agitated and has episodes of crying and wringing of hands.

Depression: Medical Perspective

John Demakis

This patient presents us with a very common problem: he is an elderly man with a significant medical disability who has lost his main means of support. Primary care physicians must frequently deal with elderly patients who have such problems. The patient has already attempted suicide once, and, because the patient readily admits that nothing in his situation has been changed, may very well attempt suicide again. The videotape leaves many things unsaid. We have no knowledge of what he was like before his first suicide attempt. Was he under the close care of a physician? Could his first suicide attempt have been predicted and prevented? We do have a record of a complete physical exam; however, it appears he is confined to a wheelchair and has significant arthritis.

I have been asked to discuss this case from the perspective of the practicing physician. Physicians usually start by eliciting a complete history, doing a physical exam, and ordering appropriate tests before beginning therapy. Because of the potential risk of suicide in this patient our approach must be altered to the following.

Recognize Suicide Risk

In approaching this case as a primary care physician, I believe that the most important action required is to recognize quickly that this patient is still a suicide risk. Patients who have previously attempted suicide are more likely to attempt suicide again than those who have never attempted suicide. In fact, sixty percent of all people who have committed suicide have made a previous suicide attempt. This fact alone should make us highly sensitive to the possibility that this patient may attempt suicide again.

The patient, however, has several other risk factors as well: He is elderly, he is a male, he shows obvious signs of depression; his wife, who had been his main support has recently died, and the patient is now living alone without a strong support system. The patient also has significant medical problems. All of these factors make this patient a high risk for a repeated suicide attempt.

In such cases, it is important for the physician to question the patient to determine if he has had thoughts of suicide. The physician should be frank but understanding. The topic may be introduced by inquiring about the patient's feeling of hopelessness and can proceed along these lines:

"Well, I see that you are feeling very low. Have you considered hurting yourself as a way out of your troubles?"

Or

"Do you sometimes feel that you would be better dead?"

If the patient acknowledges having had thoughts of suicide, the physician must learn whether the patient has plans for putting them into action.

"Do you have a specific method in mind when you might have these thoughts?"

"Have you thought about when and where you might do it?"

"Do you have a gun or are you thinking about pills or some other way of hurting yourself?"

Generally, the more concrete the patient's suicidal thoughts—his decision on a method or his selection of a specific strategy—the greater the chances that an attempt will be made.

The idea that the physician may plant suicidal ideas in a patient's mind by asking questions is unwarranted. The danger of failing to identify real suicidal intent by skipping questions about it is much more serious.

Protect the Patient

If the physician has a high suspicion that the patient is suicidal, he must act promptly and appropriately to protect the patient. If he is not already in the hospital, this patient should be hospitalized immediately. It is important that a potentially suicidal patient not be left alone but be under constant observation. If the patient is not considered a high risk for suicide, he may be left in the care of his family or friends as long as he is under constant observation. Because this patient lives alone, he should be hospitalized. A patient who has attempted suicide or who is a high risk for suicide should be referred promptly to a psychiatrist for treatment.

Contact the Family

If the physician has a suspicion that the patient may be suicidal, the family of the patient should be interviewed separately from the patient. The family can often provide additional information that can aid in his or her diagnosis and treatment.

Make the Diagnosis

Once the patient has been protected, the physician should then be able to obtain an in-depth history and a complete physical exam. At this time the physician can look for other risk factors and precipitating problems. All medical problems and medications the patient is presently taking should be carefully documented.

Treatment

Because the patient shows evidence of significant depression and has attempted suicide, he should be under the care of psychiatrist. He will probably require antidepressant medication. The primary care physician should work closely with the psychiatrist. Any medical problems should be treated.

Discharge Planning

When the patient is ready for discharge, careful consideration should be given to his living arrangements. This patient should not be allowed to move back to his trailer by himself. Other possibilities should be explored carefully with his family and friends. If suitable accommodations cannot be found with family or friends, serious consideration must be given to nursing home placement or other types of residential care programs.

Follow-up

Finally, it is important that cases such as this one have careful follow-up. The patient should be seen on a regular basis following his discharge from the hospital to make certain that things are going well, that his depression is being treated, and he has no further suicidal ideations. Follow-up is an important responsibility of the primary care physician.

In summary, if a patient has a large number of risk factors, the primary care physician should have a high index of suspicion of suicide. Once the physician has a high degree of suspicion, he must act quickly to protect the patient. Once the patient is in a protective setting, a more careful history and physical can be accomplished, in which other risk factors and precipitating problems are considered. The physician should work together with other members of the health care team to help the patient resolve these medical and social problems. Good discharge planning is essential to make sure the patient is in a protected setting. Finally, adequate follow-up is important to make sure that the support systems are working well and that the patient has no further suicidal ideations.

If the physician is suspicious of depression in a patient, an in-depth history and physical is warranted. If the physician thinks that the patient might possibly be suicidal, everything must be done to protect the patient (as discussed above). If the physician feels that suicide is not a risk, the work-up can continue:

Present History

Patients with depression frequently present a wide array of non-specific complaints. Loss of pleasure in things once enjoyed, loss of energy, or loss of initiative, are most common. Other complaints include the inability to sleep or sleeping too much, changes in eating or bowel habits, diminution or loss of sex drive, and feelings of sadness or anxiety. Patients who are depressed frequently come to the physician because of a wide array of inexplicable somatic complaints. Headache, backache, abdominal pain, and constipation without apparent cause often accompany depression. Repeated office visits or vague aches and pains for which no apparent cause can be found should raise the suspicion that the patient is depressed.

Past History

The physician should inquire carefully about previous history of depression, recent medical illness, or any medication that the patient may presently be taking. Special consideration should be given to antihypertensive medication such as reserpine, methyldopa, clonidine, and propanodol, as well as to oral contraceptives.

Social History

A careful social history should investigate family or marital problems, dramatic changes in life circumstances, financial problems, alcoholism, or recent loss of a loved one.

Family History

The family history should inquire as to whether there is a history of depression or suicide among any blood relatives.

Physical Exam

A careful physical exam will look for supporting evidence of depression, such as psychomotor retardation or agitation, as well as a sad appearance. The physical exam will also look for organic disorders that may present with depression. These include: 1) endocrine disorders such as hypothyroidism, adrenal insufficiency, and hyper-parathyroidism; 2) metabolic or nutritional disorders such as anemias due to iron, folate, or B_{12} deficiency, electrolyte disturbances, and malignancies of the pancreas or intestine; and 3) neurological disorders such as multiple sclerosis, normal pressure, hydrocephalus, and tumors of the temporal lobe.

Once the physician has diagnosed that depression exists and the patient is not suicidal, he must determine the best means of treatment. In general, if the patient shows evidence of severe depression or suicidal ideation, he should be referred to a psychiatrist. Mild to moderate depression is often treated with antidepressants. Drugs can be prescribed by a psychiatrist or, if the primary physician feels comfortable to do so, he may prescribe them himself.

If, however, depression is associated only with an adjustment disorder, such as the recent loss of a loved one or a temporary setback in his personal life, usually all the patient will require is a kind, careful, and compassionate listener. If he so wishes, the primary care physician can provide this service. Usually allowing the patient to vent, spending some time with the patient, and showing interest will carry the patient over the problem. If the primary physician feels he or she does not have the time nor the interest to provide this type of therapy, the patient should be referred to a psychologist or psychiatrist. Even with adjustment disorders, antidepressant medication may be required on a short-term basis.

If depression is thought to be secondary to medication, the medication should be adjusted or changed. If the depression is thought to be due to some secondary organic disorder, that organic disorder should be treated by the physician. Even if the depression is thought to be caused by the medication or an organic disorder, anti-depressant medication may still be indicated.

Suicide is a serious concern in our society today. At least 25,000 deaths per year in the United States are attributable to suicide. Because of the social stigma attached to death by suicide, this statistic is probably an under-reported figure. Of the many risk factors listed above for suicide, one of the most important is depression. About three-quarters of all people who actually kill themselves are depressed at the time they do so. Feelings of helplessness, hopelessness, worthlessness, or guilt about some real or imagined fault often lead to thoughts of suicide. About ten percent of all people who are severely depressed end their lives by suicide. For this reason, it is important that all health care professionals constantly be aware of the potential for suicide in their patients and be aware of the risk factors. It is also important that health care professionals be aware of the role of depression in suicidal patients and have a high index of suspicion for patients who might be depressed. Physician who are busy and forced to do rapid histories and physicals can frequently miss the diagnosis of depression in a patient. Major depression (utter hopelessness, an abiding misery, feelings of worthlessness and guilt, profound psychomotor retardation, suicidal thoughts) is often easy to diagnose. However, minor depression and reactive depression may be far more subtle and more difficult to diagnose unless the physician is willing to spend more time with the patient, be a good listener, and have a high index of suspicion.

In summary, depression is a common problem that is often unrecognized by non-psychiatric physicians. Patients rarely admit that they are depressed, and the signs and symptoms may be subtle. Yet, with a high degree of suspicion and careful listening, a physician can usually make the diagnosis. Severe depression or depression with suicidal thoughts should be referred to a psychiatrist. Mild depression or depression associated with adjustment disorders may be treated by the primary care physician or referred to a psychologist or psychiatrist.

Depression: Psychological Perspective

Nicholas D. Kokonis

The sight of this 80-year-old, widowed, depressed man in a wheelchair is a sight of utter despair. I see in this old man a case of agitated depression—a state of helplessness, hopelessness, worthlessness, and self-accusation. Feeling unloved, possibly rejected, this man is experiencing what psychologists have called an "existential vacuum."

When faced with such a patient, one asks, "Is there a purpose in depressed behavior, a struggle to accomplish something that will improve his situation and reduce the force of his distress?" When I work with a depressed individual, I like to reconstruct his whole life pattern so as to have a better understanding of the forces that have impacted upon him. I like to interpret the man's spell of depression as a reaction to loss: the loss of a loved person or a congenial group or supportive system. The loss might be of a more subtle, symbolic nature. Regardless of who the person, group, institution was, the significance of the loss is in the fact that it reanimates terrible childhood experiences that have to do with the loss of the mother's affection. And so, in this old man's depression there is a meaning: In this man's hell of mental illness, I see a cry for love and a cry for meaning. I see a display of helplessness and a direct appeal for the affection and security that have been lost in losing his wife. The agitated depression syndrome, which I believe clearly describes the behavior and emotional dynamics of this man, perhaps needs a little bit further explanation. It is a state of mind in which thoughts of death are prominent and suicide is a real danger.

Patients who suffer from agitated depression cannot keep still, cannot sleep, can only pace up and down, often moaning and sighing, ringing their hands or pulling their hair. The very existence of this syndrome, this variant form of clinical depression, makes it clear to us clinicians that dejected moods and underactivity do not necessarily go together. Agitated depression seems to combine *depressed* mood and *anxious* tension.

However, this picture of depression is complicated by the angry hostility that is directed against the deserting person—in this case, this man's wife—and by guilty fear that this hostility has actually caused the desertion. In the psychological evolution of symptoms, repentance soon gains the upper hand, so to speak, and the rage turns against the self. The patient becomes very self-critical, and his unending self-criticism being intended as an act of expiation. He will fully accept the blame for the anger and then confess his unworthiness and attempt to deserve again and win back the lost affection.

However, in many patients these emotional tactics are likely to miscarry. The self-punishment becomes very painful and the despair unbearable, even driving the patient to suicide, before the attempted expiation brings any sense of restored love.

The spell of depression can be conceived as the man's attempt, however misdirected, to repair the situation that has been created by the serious loss of supporting love. And so, in the present disease, we have a situation that is like a drama whose first acts have been played before the lights have gone up on the stage.

Studies of depressed patients indicate that a vulnerable point exists in the organization of their personalities: They are very dependent upon their principal "love object." They show an acute dependence on a high income of supportive love and affection and cannot tolerate frustration or disappointment from this source. They require, it seems, a constant supply of love and moral support from a highly valued love object. This requirement creates a weakness in their personality makeup that affects their sense of competence. As children, they show a special need for the approval of others. When young, they seem to develop a technique by means of which they obtain approval rather than developing a sense of self-worth or self-esteem that might have sustained them in the years ahead, especially in the young adult and adult years.

This man's crisis is at once a psychological, social, and spiritual crisis. He probably is experiencing a certain empty frustration that life has no meaning at this point. Faced with the unavoidable—suffering, dying—this man is probably experiencing what Eric Erikson calls *despair*. As he looks back upon his life as a series of missed opportunities and misdirections, now, in his twilight years, he probably realizes that it is too late to start again. For him, the inevitable result is a sense of despair at what might have been. His personality lacks the necessary strength to face his predicament. In this regard, he is not like Socrates, Ghandi, or even Martin Luther King, who said almost one the eve of his assassination, "I don't mind—my eyes have seen the promised land." Instead, this man cries for love and support; he cannot do alone.

In working with an individual like this man, one is especially reminded of the fact that health and happiness, as well as disease and disability, derive not only from man's bodily constitution and the physical environment in which he lives, but also from his psychological and behavioral interactions with the people who in his family, neighborhood and state comprise his social world. To thrive, human beings must draw upon certain "psychological supplies," such as attention, affection, approval, and control. Without an appropriate balance of these supplies, man may suffer from forms of "psychosocial malnutrition" that can produce results as disastrous to his health as physical malnutrition induced by dietary imbalances.

But there is a very significant difference between material resources and psychosocial supplies. The fact that most material resources can be held in the hand, weighed, and analyzed by physical means has made them relatively easy to recognize, characterize, and measure with scientific precision. Psychosocial supplies, on the other hand, pose a problem because they comprise various forms of interpersonally transmitted information concerning such matters as being valued, being the object of attention, being controlled, and being reasonably secure about continuing to receive these supplies in the future. It is the recipient who decides whether he is being valued, attended to, controlled, and so forth. The fact that this decision is not always made evident to an outside observer by the behavior of the recipient may at times pose difficulties for the clinician/diagnostician.

Now, to some facts: Depression is the most common psychiatric disorder treated in office practice and in out-patient clinics. Some authorities have estimated that at least 12% of the adult population will have an episode of depression of sufficient clinical severity to warrant treatment. Prompt diagnosis and treatment of this condition is obviously a measure of health concern. Complete recovery from an episode of depression occurs in 70 to 95% of the cases. About 25% of the younger patients recover completely. After the initial attack of depression, 47 to 79% of the patients will have a recurrence at some time in their life. After the first such type of depression, most patients have a symptom-free interval of more than three years before the next attack. However, approximately 5% of hospitalized manic-depressive patients subsequently commit suicide. The notion that the patient who threatens suicide will not carry out the threat is fallacious.

And how should depression be treated?

Medical therapy for depression is at least as ancient as Homer, who related in the *Odyssey* that Penelope took a drug to dull her grief for her long-absent husband. However, as a psychologist, I am particularly interested in psychotherapy, or the psychological treatment of depression. For this point of view, I would recommend the following steps:

First, the precipitating or aggravating environmental factors that may be blocking the patient's effort to rest or to relax should be removed.

Second, the patient should be helped to become aware that inordinate conscientiousness stems from inner feelings of guilt, from an over-strict conscience, and from keen feelings of insecurity. He should be encouraged to expect less of himself and then to develop a more nonchalant outlook on life.

Third, in addition to re-education, reassurance, and explanation, the clinician should also explain that the illness is self-limiting and that the person will get well. Advice should be given to the family and friends. It should be explained that the illness requires rest and relaxation and that the patient must avoid anything that increases his tension and anxiety. Occupational therapy and bibliotherapy are also likely to prove very helpful. The patient should be encouraged to read, to relax and to improve his mind and personality. I very often recommend that my patients read in the Bible, as I have personally found that to be a very comforting experience. I maintain a list of bibliotherapeutic references, and I share this with my patients when appropriate. My psychotherapy program is individualized according to the patient, the phase of his illness, and the intensity of the symptoms. I am almost certain that depressed individuals need to be understood, need to develop their hope, and need to be supported. Therefore, supportive psychotherapy, as contrasted to insight-oriented or exploratory psychotherapy, is likely to be more helpful with very depressed individuals. Reassurance venting, catharsis, guidance, and environmental changes are among the techniques I rely upon. In a case like that of this individual, I would also consider hospitalization as an extreme form of environmental change.

In my frequent contacts with an individual who is as depressed as this man, I would be guided by the precept that suffering ceases to be suffering in some way at the moment that it finds meaning. Physical remedies and treatments are of immense value. Psychotherapy is a new field through which many distressed individuals have found healing, but the therapist and the patient by themselves integrate the individual's personality, for neither can relate it to reality. One of the healthiest performances of a man's life is the performance in which, even though it be through utter despair or through the persistence of restlessness that can find no other satisfaction, he turns himself toward God and begins to quest for the One who has been seeking Him all his life. Indeed, man's restlessness is a sign of that search. One of the basic tenets of one form of psychotherapy called *logotherapy* is that man's main concern is not to gain pleasure or to avoid pain but to see a meaning in his life. This reason explains why a man is ever ready to suffer with the condition that his suffering has meaning. In this regard, I know no wiser and no truer words in the world that the words of St. Augustine: "Unquiet is our heart until it rests in Thee."

Depression: Theological Perspective

Nicholas Krommydas

Our Lord came into this world to "bear the infirmities" of us all. If He indeed was Christ, one of His outward signs would be to heal the sick.

In Matthew 4:24 we read, "So his fame spread throughout all Syria and they brought him all the sick, those afflicted with various diseases and pains, demoniacs, epileptics and paralytics and he healed them."

Christ's healings were a demonstration both of His Divinity and of His mercy and love for man. So that the power that He brought into the world should not to be lost with His Ascension into Heaven. He commands His disciples and follow-ers: "Heal the sick, cleanse the lepers, raise the dead, cast out devils; freely ye have received, freely give" (Matt. 10:8). This power has been and remains in the Church through the Holy Spirit and continues through disciples, priests, and all those who are called to administer the true healing that God can only bring (Mark 6:13).

Throughout the centuries, those who have understood Christ's command and His charge of healing have been given the special gift of the restoration of health in His name. They are the Spiritual Fathers and Directors who have followed their Master totally and have therefore received the Grace to carry out this awesome command.

The spiritual father in our Christian tradition is the equivalent of the modern doctor-counsellor. He is not just a knowledgeable individual, but one who lives in the very presence of Christ, having experienced the healing power of God. He is the one who by example, compassion, and love seeks to bring those who suffer to the one true Physician.

I would therefore like to elaborate first on what the traditional Orthodox understanding of Spiritual Direction is, and then sketch some of the basic characteristics that a spiritual father should possess, and finally, make some brief comments on the case of depression described in light of these comments.

St. Basil says that for every ailment there is a cure. Our God is a Healing God, as Scripture clearly and repeatedly shows. A spiritual director—"Abba," or spiritual father, "gerontas"—is one who has had a first-hand experience of healing in His life, as a result of his relationship with Christ—the true healer. This person is girded with the gift of transmitting God's healing power within the faith.

The tradition of the Fathers, especially of the Desert Fathers, was that its if one is not touched by brokenness, it is difficult to heal brokenness. Thus, the spiritual director is constantly, actively, vigilantly, listening to the promptings of the Holy Spirit as he hears—or rather lives—the pain of the one who suffers.

When we come in touch with the Holy Spirit, we realize that its main purpose is to divinize—to lift the *whole* person as one—body, mind, soul—and help it to become whole, or integrated.

The Church encourages this process of spiritual direction because in this very special relationship of Spiritual Father/Spiritual Son or Director/Directee, the individual works out his or her need, but also becomes sensitive to God's Grace and the spiritual challenge of life.

The Fathers of our Church emphasized that man needs God and His Grace. When one grows distant from Him, when one drifts, then sin and all its attributes rush in. We thus need healing and metanoia—a return, a change of heart— whereby we realize that at our innermost self, *we crave* God. In our Orthodox Faith we can say that we crave not just an abstract God but one who loves and has compassion for us such that He gives Himself and of Himself. Therefore, we always conclude and yearn for the Parousia—the Kingdom—the presence, and the synergy of being together with God, whereby we are united in one with Him.

A *spiritual director* is not a professional in the sense of the word, but rather one who is grounded in humility, charity, openness, and love. He ought to be rooted in the spirit of God and the Divine. His aim is to bring others to God and thus introduce them to salvation, which can only come from God. He ought to love deeply and take on others' suffering as His own. He can only do this because he is anchored in God and can thus bring healing to that which ails. In his relationship with others, he does not try to solve problems, but tries rather to create a relationship of love and attentiveness to God's Spirit in order that it becomes the soil— the arena —where true healing takes place. The word *compassion* means entering into one's suffering; and this word above all expresses the Spiritual Father's domain.

Although he incorporates various skills and techniques learned from other disciplines, the true gift of the spiritual father is *diakrisis*—discernment and concern as to the workings of God's Spirit within us, thus revealing the true state of our Spiritual being. We can therefore say that direction is form-free, using Scripture, the Tradition of the Fathers, the Church, and knowledge from other areas to lead one to *wholeness* and to "the knowledge of truth".

All these actions take place within a certain context—the Church. The Church is the true place where we become true listeners of God's voice. The Church is the people of God witnessing to the active presence of God in history. It is there where we are reminded of what is really happening. In its yearly cycle of events it unfolds to us the Christ event and keeps us rooted in God by making His active presence known to us. It is there where the healing power of the Spirit can be mystically received, especially in the form of the sacraments and by the fact that we belong to Christ's Body—His Church—His Community.

Comments on Depression

I have tried to set the stage whereby we are able to differentiate between the various disciplines in response to a cry for healing. By no means is the religious isolated or insulated from other disciplines. As a matter of fact, I would strongly recommend both medical and/or psychological assistance for the man in this particular case.

It is important to provide for those in need by individuals who share and understand God's healing process. Most times, referrals become divisive and suggest that only one method of healing is available or possible, therefore blocking a true and total healing of the whole person.

I would like to point out the following:

1) That the person came to the priest and his church and therefore has certain expectations and trusts that healing can come from there (i.e., Christ, the Church);

2) That the person has taken a step towards facing a problem, discussing openly his depression, therefore remaining open to receiving direction—forgiveness, the sacraments, and the support of a Christian community—the church;

3) Because he has chosen to come to the Church and he is familiar with the various ways that healing is administered—through Holy Communion, confession, unction, prayer, and so forth—this knowledge can be of assistance to him;

4) The link that will make all this happen and bring him true healing—by intro-
ducing him to the true healer of body-soul—is the *Spiritual Father*, whose
knowledge and skills in various disciplines will support his recovery and
whose love, concern, and compassion will see to it that he is directed not to a
particular person or method of healing only, but to a true and total saving of
his soul. Spiritual guidance in this case and in all cases is not just crisis intervention, but a continuous process, the movement to God and in God.

Part Four

AIDS and Cancer: The Role of the Helping Professionals

Human Immunodeficiency Virus (HIV) Infections and Acquired Immunodeficiency Syndrome (AIDS): Impact on Lifestyles in the Twenty-first Century

George J. Pazin

INTRODUCTION

The closer one gets to the HIV-AIDS problem, the greater one's concern grows, not only because of AIDS but also because of the impact it will have in the future. As the epidemic spreads, more people are being brought closer to the problem, and its ramifications looms larger for everyone.

Although medicine, and virology in particular, has made remarkable progress in the past few decades, it is not apparent whether a vaccine, a cure, or even a highly effective therapy for HIV infections and AIDS will be forthcoming in the near future. Clearly, as the twenty-first century approaches, HIV infections and AIDS have already had a great impact upon many lives and lifestyles, and it seems likely that they will continue to do so in an even more dramatic fashion.

My expertise lies in the area of microbiological infectious diseases, which gives me a medical perspective on the problem but any thoughtful physician must realize that the current AIDS problem has psychological and spiritual dimensions as well. Therefore, I will share with you my insights from all three perspectives.

THE MEDICAL PERSPECTIVE

Virological Aspects

When dealing with a disease caused by a virus, it is critically important not to overlook the virus itself. In the case of AIDS, the virus that causes the disease is human immunodeficiency virus, or HIV. It is surprising, but apparently true, that HIV is a relatively new virus. The earliest evidence of the virus comes from a few positive blood samples drawn in central Africa in 1959. In the United States, there is evidence that a few person were infected with HIV in 1978. (A single case was reported to have tested positive for the HIV as early as 1969 and has received nationwide media publicity, but the case has not been reported officially in medical literature.)

Let's digress for a few moments in order to answer a few questions regarding viruses.

What is a virus? Simply stated, a virus is a sub-microscopic "package of chemicals" that has genetic material in the center and is surrounded by a protective coat with or without a lipid, or fatty, envelope on the outside. The HIV happens to have this outer envelope. It helps one to understand viral infections if one realizes that viruses are not alive.

If viruses are not alive, how do they function? The virus does nothing outside a cell. However, if it attaches itself to an appropriate cell, it fuses with that cell. Once inside, the genetic material of the virus redirects the cell to make virus instead of the usual things a cell needs to remain alive. The viral takeover of the cell is injurious and often results in cell death. If enough cells die, the whole body is damaged. In the case of HIV, the virus infects and destroys the key cell in the immune system which ordinarily protects the body from infections and tumors.

So why does it matter that HIV infections and AIDS are caused by a virus? Viruses are transmissible from person to person. However, because they are not alive, viruses tend to be passively transferred. Viruses such as HIV, which have lipid envelopes, become inactivated rather easily outside the body, especially if they become dried out.

The main cell infected by HIV is a cell in the blood, so it appears that the HIV must gain access to the blood to infect a person. Thus, HIV is not highly contagious but, on the other hand, it may spread during a single exposure if its properly inoculated. Because viruses execute their damage within cells, it is quite difficult to inhibit viral reproduction selectively without damaging other cells in the body. Surprising progress has been made with respect to therapy directed against HIV, but it is clear that treatment involving zidovudine (Retrovir, formerly called azidothymidine or AZT) is only partially effective. HIV is a difficult virus to make into an effective vaccine, and it is not clear whether an effective vaccine can be made at all.

The Medical Aspect

As noted above, HIV attaches to and fuses with the key cell in the immune system—the system that acts as the body's protection against infections and cancers. As a result, many persons who are infected with HIV become highly susceptible to severe, life-threatening infections or unusual forms of cancer. Not everyone who is infected with HIV develops AIDS, but of those who develop AIDS, not one has had his/her immune system return to normal, with the possible exception of one patient with AIDS who received a bone marrow transplant from an identical twin. Although we may treat some of the infections or cancers for a time, most persons with AIDS succumb within two to three years.

All persons who are infected with AIDS are potentially *able to infect* persons with whom they share blood, body fluids, or tissues, regardless or whether they have developed AIDS or remain asymptomatic.

Infectious Disease Aspect

AIDS would be a fearsome disease if it were of unknown etiology, but the fact that it is caused by an infectious agent that is transmissible from person to person adds an important element that complicates disease control. The transmissibility of the causative virus contributes to the public's concerns and, to some extent, to its hostility.

Although the spread of HIV creates a major social health concern, an understanding of what is involved in the spread of infectious agents enables people to avoid the infection. In general, the spread of infectious agents such as HIV involves: 1) exposure to the virus; 2) its inoculation into the body; and 3) one's susceptibility to the virus. Operationally, until a vaccine is developed (and we should not depend upon this happening), everyone must be considered susceptible to HIV at any time.

The two elements involved with spread of infections that are modifiable are *exposure* to and *inoculation* with HIV. Exposure is necessary, but not sufficient, to establish an infection. If one avoids exposure to the virus, one does not need to worry about preventing inoculation. However, one may not be totally able to avoid exposure to the virus. Fortunately, inoculation is an important additional factor that determines whether exposure may lead to infection. With respect to HIV inoculation is usually accomplished when the virus is forced into the body through the skin or lining surfaces during sexual intimacy or via the injection of virus into the body during the kind of needle sharing associated with intravenous drug abuse. Receiving contaminated blood, blood products or organs directly into the body are

George J. Pazin

relatively uncommon, but important, additional means of becoming infected with HIV.

The behaviors associated with male homosexuality and intravenous drug abuse provide both the exposure *and* inoculation requirements for the spread of HIV, but these requirements can also definitely be present during *heterosexual* behavior as well.

Although casual or close personal contact with an HIV-infected person may result in exposure to the virus, if inoculation does not occur, one does not become infected. On the other hand, unprotected sexual relations with an infected person is clearly risky. Exactly where the dividing line is between casual or close personal contact and intimate sexual contact is not addressed very often. In my opinion, intimate contact is present at that point where HIV in a body fluid may be inoculated directly upon a mucosal membrane or lining surface, such as the inside of the mouth. Therefore, during passionate kissing, it might be possible for the virus to be transferred from an infected person to an uninfected person if the mucosal lining is inoculated. Whether the virus can be spread by passionate kissing remains an unanswered question, but I feel that the seriousness of AIDS or HIV infection (serious in terms of its contagiousness as well as its potential for disease) dictates that it must be assumed that the spread of HIV via passionate kissing is possible and must not be ignored in our efforts to avoid infection with HIV.

The Medical Impact of HIV Infection and AIDS on Lifestyles

One's *premium* should be to avoid exposure to and perhaps even more importantly, to avoid *inoculation* to HIV. The medical significance of this infection dictates that thoughtful people should have *"risk elimination not risk reduction"* as their goal. Although latex prophylactics may provide an effective barrier to the genital exchange of body fluids containing HIV, direct exchange of saliva containing HIV may provide the functional equivalent of a "small leak." It seems, therefore, medically advisable to reserve passionate kissing to serious or monogamous relationships, not promiscuous ones. Most public health-minded physician have concluded that casual sexual relations are not advisable in many areas of our country. A conservative approach would also question the advisability of "casual passionate petting." Medically speaking, courting should become more and more thoughtful, deliberate, and geared in "slow motion" rather than to the casual, "anything goes," "let's try it" attitudes that prevailed in the sexual revolution of the 1960s and 1970s.

THE PSYCHOLOGICAL PERSPECTIVE

Two events during the 1960s had a profound effect upon the collective psyche of American society. The development of the oral contraceptive and the landing on the moon gave Americans an attitude that "anything goes in without consequence"

Psycho-Social Issues in Caring for Persons with AIDS: A Theological Perspective

Peter Poulos

Theological Framework

Although my presentation today is being given to a group of physicians, psychologists, psychiatrists, social workers, other health professionals and clergy, I would like to begin by talking briefly about theology. It is basic for me—and I would hope for each of us, regardless of the particular type of ministry we are engaged in—to have some sense of what my Orthodox background brings and how it influences the way that I approach and see people in my hospital work. So, I would like to set the stage for my reflections on AIDS by sharing briefly some of what I would emphasize in my theology and in my work.

For me, the basic teaching of Orthodoxy is that the human person is made in the "image and likeness of God"—the belief that when we approach people and look at people, His image is what we are looking at. I have said to student-chaplains, "I don't care if she is a prostitute or whether she is brought to the Emergency Room on Saturday at 3:00 a.m.; if you are going to minister to her, you have to have some sense of her being made in the image and likeness of God, even if *she* doesn't know it."

What does this mean, "the image and likeness of God"? I think that, as we study about God, get to know God, and relate with God, we get to know more of what it means to be human because we *are* made in the image and likeness of God. I am not saying that being human is the same as being God. But we can sense and learn some of that potential we have of being fully human by getting closer to and knowing God.

What are some of these things that we learn about God? *God is love.* To love! Love is basic to what it means to relate as human beings. *God is the Creator.* If you have ever watched children making things, you have seen the thrill they have. "Look what I made!" they say. We all have some of that creative drive. When we do gardening, carpentry, art work, cooking, baking, we have a sense of being part of that creative role.

Our God has relationships with others. We see this in the different persons of the Holy Trinity—Father, Son, and Holy Spirit—and in the different role each has and in how they relate. God, also has relationship with people; He has made a covenant with people. *God has a relationship to the Church or the Church as community.* St. Paul tells us "to bear one another's burdens and so fulfill the law of Christ." Living in that kind of relationship is basic to who we are. When we move away from those things—those God-like things—we live in sin—not sin against some God who is up in the sky, but sin against the way we were made to live. I often use the phrase "we sin against ourselves," which leads to illness and suffering. The emphasis in the Orthodox spiritual life is to live in relationship to the Holy Spirit, experiencing the presence of the Holy Spirit and being influenced by it more and more. This relationship is a very personal one, basic to human life and to the Orthodox Christian life.

There is in the Judaeo-Christian tradition a theme that takes on more meaning for me the more I am faced with problems or crises related to change in people's lives. This theme is the theme of Death & Resurrection—moving through that death-like exile or wilderness to new life. The ancient Greek philosopher, Heraclitus, taught that everything in life changes.

That teaching is a basic truth about life. Much of our Church's ritual ministers to people at a point of significant change in their lives—weddings, baptisms (which minister not just to the infant but to the parents, who are in a process of change), and funerals (which are not just for the deceased but minster to the experience of loss felt by both family and friends). Every major human experience is a movement away from one thing and toward something else. Our belief in death and resurrection can influence how we face those changes.

A final theological emphasis deals with values and worth. Where do we derive our value and worth? From how much money we make? From how physically attractive we are? From how popular we are? From our position? From what we do? Is it our actions that give us value worth? Or is it the fact that we are children of God, made in the image and likeness God? Our value and worth come not from what we do or what we have but from who we are!

These tenets are basic for me as I approach patients in the hospital or care for people's needs. Who is it I am going to see? My belief that we are all children of God influences what I am doing, how I am listening, and what I am hearing.

The Person with AIDS

Now let us look at some of the particular concerns related to persons who have AIDS. It is instructive to look at the change that occur in an AIDS patient's various relationships to understand the psycho-social concerns inherent in the problem. These relationships seem to change immediately upon a diagnosis of AIDS.

Relationship to Oneself

The relationship of a person who has AIDS to him or herself changes upon a diagnosis of AIDS. (If I refer to persons who have AIDS as *him*, please forgive me. I know that women now how AIDS, but until recently most have been men, so please let the masculine pronoun refer to both.) Actually, even people who don't have AIDS but whose HIV blood test comes back positive, showing that they've been exposed to AIDS also experience a change in their relationship to themselves. They have a sense of uncertainty, of not knowing what that positive blood test really means. They wonder if they will develop the disease. Uncertainty—that sense of the unknown—now becomes part of their life. If they catch a cold, they become frightened that it is AIDS.

When a person does develop AIDS, he can experience a drastic change in how he sees himself—in his self-image. Suddenly, the reality of death, which we are so good at keeping at a distance, now becomes part of his life. It now becomes a real threat! Rather quickly, from having been a strong young man, he begins to feel and look old. How many patients have said that: "I have lost so much weight, often as much as 80 pounds, and I am always so exhausted that I feel like a very old man." That sense of himself as being young, strong, powerful, invulnerable is gone.

Most people who are young value their ability to work and to be independent. However, as he becomes more ill he will at some point have to stop work and begin to depend on others for assistance. He may need to go on Medicaid, Supplemental Security income, or other public assistance. At first, with the back and forth quality of AIDS, he may not be strong enough to work but not so sick that he needs to stay in bed or even at home. It is hard for him to place himself. "Am I sick or am I not sick? They tell me I have AIDS, but some days I feel like myself again! They must have made a mistake. I don't have AIDS." This kind of dialogue with himself can continue until the person gets much sicker.

A person who is diagnosed as having AIDS is often in the position of having to tell others, for the first time, that he is gay or about his use, even if it is in the past, of IV drugs. He can feel exposed, as if his privacy were stripped away.

Something that the person was able to keep private before is now generally known.

It is not unusual in times of crisis and hardship to try to explain why something has happened. When ill, people often ask, "Why am I being punished like this? What did I do to cause this?" I think that some of this questioning is an effort to regain some sense of control over one's life again. Not knowing *why* can be frightening. With a diagnosis of AIDS, a person often blames himself.

The two most difficult issues that each of us has to face in our development are *sexuality and death* (i.e., mortality). Most of us have to struggle to come to terms with our fascination with or attraction to and fear of both. The AIDS patient who is gay has to deal with both of these issues together. It is not unusual, even for a person who appeared to be comfortable with his sexual identity, to begin to feel that illness is a punishment for his sexuality: "I am being punished because I am sexual" or "I am being punished because I am gay." Even that part of himself that he thought was settled now becomes an issue again.

The other day, I was visiting with a 75-year-old physician who is a patient of mine. He has been battling cancer for seven years but always bounced back to the point that he could continue his now small practice.

Now, suddenly however, he was becoming much weaker. On the day I visited him and his wife, his attending physician came to inform them that the cancer had now spread to the liver. The physician-patient was told that he probably had a matter of weeks to months to live. As the couple reacted to this news, talking about their life together and expressing the hope for more time, the patient said something that struck me: "I want more time—I hope and pray for it—but if I don't get it, at least I had 75 years." I have never met an AIDS patient who could say this. Most are faced with death as a rude interruption—a rude ending much too early in their lives. I don't know if death has a proper order or time in anyone's life, but with most AIDS patients, it seems out of order—and much too early—and turns the order of life upside down.

Relationship with One's Family

One's relationship with his family, and the relationships within the family, change upon a diagnosis of AIDS.

It is out of order for parents to bury children! And having to deal with their child's sexual identity is often thrust upon them at the same moment that his probable death is.

Family reactions vary widely. One father stood in the doorway of his son's hospital room, stared at his son, and then yelled, "You faggot" and ran away. However, that patient's mother and sister remained as a support to him, a situation that is not unusual.

Jim was a 35-year-old man who had elderly parents. He had lived in New York for a few years. He was raised in a small town where his father had served as minister in a conservative fundamentalist Church. After he told his parents and his brother and sister-in-law that he was gay and that he had AIDS, Jim's brother never talked to him again. When Jim would call, his sister-in-law would make an excuse why her husband was not available. She sometimes would telephone Jim to see how he was; her husband never did. When Jim's parents wanted to come to New York to visit him while he was hospitalized, he said no. Jim found all kinds of excuses why they should not come. When we talked about it one day, he got angry at me and said, "Look, it's not as if we were ever close." Yet Jim never failed to tell me when his mother had called. It meant something to him. Jim tended to be a real loner—a generally depressed type of guy, which is what concerned me.

After he was discharged from the hospital, he did allow his parents to come to New York to visit. A friend of his, who drove Jim to the airport to greet them, later told me that Jim would not even let his mother hug him.

Some families really stay by the patient and are supportive. Even these families, however, have some special considerations or issues peculiar to AIDS. Joe, a 30-year-old former IV drug user, was diagnosed as having AIDS when he became very ill with *Pneumocystis Carinii* pneumonia. His wife, parents, sisters, and brothers stood by him as he ran high fevers. The sister to whom he first turned for help, seems especially close to him. Now that he is home, she visits regularly. She will not eat or drink, however, from anything but a paper cup or paper plate when she goes to her brother's home. She allows him to visit her house but serves him only on paper plates and paper cups. She's very frightened. Her brother understands and says he does not mind. He appreciate that she is there for him. His wife, however, is furious and tells her sister-in-law that if she really loved her brother, she would not do this. I suspect that what the wife is really angry at is not the use of paper goods but that her husband turned first to his sister for support. Families have their own histories and ways of relating to each other, which becomes part of the dynamic as they react to AIDS in the family.

One of the things that Joe's sister is struggling with, by the way, is that she has never lost a close relative to death. The thought that her brother, who is five years younger than she, will die soon is something she cannot imagine. Death is coming close and invading her boundaries, her space, and it is threatening.

The other thing that she and the rest of the family struggle with is what to tell people. Cousins, friends, and others not in the immediate family have been told that he has cancer, with no mention of AIDS. His parents are especially ashamed of it and would not want all the relatives to know. Imagine knowing that your family is ashamed of you!

The sister is concerned that no one in her neighborhood learn that her brother has AIDS. She has two young daughters and is afraid the other mothers will not allow their children to play with her children if they knew the uncle has AIDS.

Her concern is not surprising. Just the other day three young brothers in Florida—ages 8, 9 & 10—returned for the first time in a year to their elementary school. All three boys are hemophiliacs who exhibited antibodies to the AIDS virus in their blood. Their parents had to get a court order to get them back in school. The school officials and other parents had barred them from school. These kids didn't even have the disease—just the antibodies in their blood.

Relationships to Friends and Significant Others in the Lives of AIDS Patients

Unfortunately, sometimes friends run away. That should not be surprising. Everyone wants to run away from death; that is a natural initial reaction. The reason that some people run when a friend has been diagnosed as having AIDS is that it comes too close to home. If people pall around together, do the same things, why does one get AIDS and not the other. One feels guilty that he is well and his friend is sick. He may feel frightened because he looks at his friend and wonders when it will be his turn. When I hear some gay men talk about the number of their friends who have died from AIDS, I am amazed. It is frightening! They must spend a lot of their time going to funerals—in the same way that many elderly people do—which forces them to confront these issues constantly.

It should be said that while some friends may abandon someone who has AIDS, many do not. In many cases, because the person with AIDS does not live near family or may not want to go back to family or be welcomed there, it is his friends who take care of him. A friend may even move in or invite the AIDS victim to stay with him. The friend shops and cooks for him, takes him to the doctor, and is there to talk with him.

An excellent book entitled *When Someone You Know Has AIDS: A Practical Guide* by Leonard Martelli with Fran Peltz and William Messina has been published recently. Parts of this book make readers cry as they read how supportive some "care partners," as they are referred to, are.

The care partners are there through all the mood swings that a person with AIDS goes through, and they go through some or their own. These people need to be helped to recognize that it is not unusual for very sick people to express most of their anger at those who are closest to them. Perhaps the AIDS victims feel that they can trust these people to come back to them; they can't be sure that doctors or people who are not so close to them will. These care partners are not necessarily "lovers," although some are. The bond that grows between person who has AIDS and his care partner is a beautiful thing to see. When they learn to be open with each other about their feelings, whatever they are feeling, a real bond develops. It can be a time of growth, of new experience for both. I mentioned earlier that confronting death often brings new life, new discovery. That loner, Jim, whom I talked about earlier, learned to become more open with his friends, to let them in, to accept their help. This openness was very new for him. It enriched the last year of his life not to feel so isolated and alone.

Gays show a greater sense of community than IV drug users have. Drug users seem unable to give each other as much support as do gays.

Again, an issue or concern that is often difficult for someone caring for a person with AIDS is how much can he tell other people. Can a care partner tell his boss and co-workers why he may be tired or appear pre-occupied? Can he tell them why he has to rush home after work? It is difficult when someone is taking so much of the care person's physical and emotional energy, and yet he may have to keep that information hidden. Imagine if a spouse were seriously ill and in the process of dying, and yet the other spouse must keep that secret from his co-workers and acquaintances?

Where do people with AIDS get their support? Fortunately, there are support groups. Some New York City hospitals that have large numbers of AIDS patients and are adequately staffed offer separate support groups for the patients and their care partners. The Gay Men's Health Crisis in New York started this support system and offers many supportive services to persons with AIDS and their care partners.

The Relationships with Medical Personnel and Hospital Staff

In 1980, we had in our Clinical Pastoral Education Program an Episcopal priest who lived in Greenwich Village. He talked then about a disease that was hitting a number of gay males in that community. He said that he spent many evenings ministering at St. Vincent's Hospital in Greenwich Village because people who lived in that community and knew he was a priest would ask him to visit friends and loved ones. I must confess that I did not fully believe him. He brought in an article entitled "The Gay Plague," which talked about this mysterious illness. I did not believe him until he began to cry as he talked about what it was like seeing some many young men die.

Now I believe him because we all cry. AIDS is no longer the gay plague, and it is no longer in just some hospitals. We all see it in our hospitals nows.

By the way, the gay community has some anger against, and perhaps some mistrust of, the medical world because it has taken so long for society as a whole to recognize the AIDS problem. I have to admit that I feel guilty for doubting that priest in 1980. It amazed me that this crisis could have been going on in one community, just a short distance away, and we did not know about it.

Today, we are all bombard with talk of AIDS. It makes us feel threatened and frightened. The same is true of hospital staffs. We have had situations in my hospital where an AIDS patient's food was being left at his door because the hospital worker was afraid to go in. As we looked into that problem, we saw how frightened some staff members were to have any contact with AIDS patients. One could see a clear difference between how caring nurses could be on some floors and how distant they could be on floors that had AIDS patients. Education regarding precautions helped this situation. In some cases, though, a lot of what was getting in the way of the hospital workers' care was not so much fear of contagion but judgement and condemnation.

Comments about AIDS patients who were gay or who were IV drug users—how they had brought this on themselves—could be heard everywhere. Some of this paranoia was part of a sexuality phobia. I think that some of us are raised with this fear of that tiger called sexuality—that if we let it run loose, it will destroy us. Behind some of the staff members' concern was the need to blame: "They did it! They let it run loose and they are being punished." I have tried to help some staff members who have expressed such feelings and beliefs to look at what they are saying. Is God punishing AIDS victims? Is God punishing the little infant who is born HIV positive, suffers, and dies? I think that hospitals need to look at the toll that caring for persons with AIDS has on their staffs, especially on nurses. There is already a national shortage of nurses; add to that the strain of caring for young people who are dying, and you have a very stressful situation.

In regard to the stress related to fear of contagion, I believe that we need to distinguish between real threat and exaggerated threat. I have caught myself at times stepping back when an AIDS patient begins to cough. Without thinking, I move back. Then I think, "Why did I do that?" On an intellectual level, I know I cannot catch AIDS by being in a room with an AIDS patient who coughs. Yet on an emotional level, I feel threatened. However, this threat is only imaginary or exaggerated. Surgeons, on the other hand, will tell you about the real threat they face when performing surgery on a patient who might have AIDS. There is a real danger if a surgeon were accidentally to jab his finger when an AIDS patient's blood is all over. One can take precautions, of course, but does one take them with all patients? It can slow doctors down. Emergency Room Staff respond to patients in crisis who are sometimes brought in with nothing known about their medical history. These are some concerns that hospital staff are now addressing because of the AIDS problem. They are facing situations that they have never had to face before.

One thing I have noticed in facing new situations is that sometimes we have to re-examine some of our stereotyped images. We are seeing that not all people with a history of IV drug use are uneducated people who have alienated themselves from their families. We are seeing that not all gays are effeminate hairdressers. We have even seen some gay couples where the partner stands by the dying patient like any other spouse would. The bond in the relationship may be strong. The amount of understanding and support they often have for each other is surprising.

We need to acknowledge these positive elements in a gay relationship even when we may not be comfortable with the gay lifestyle. As the patient becomes more ill, the partner will need to be included in discussions that influence the patient's in-hospital and post-discharge care.

I want to emphasize that we are all facing a very threatening new situation. I believe it is extremely important that we listen to the feelings and concerns of our patients, their families, and loved one—and to our own feelings and concerns as well. We have not been in this place before. It is new and uncertain. Let us admit that we are anxious and frightened. Let us explore these feelings and not punish ourselves or others for them. Let us not let our anxiety and fear cause us to relate to any person, including ourselves, without recognizing the value and worth of every person made in the image and likeness of God.

AIDS: Is it a Moral Crisis?

Milton B. Efthimiou

Society

"From its first appearance, the disease inspired an almost hysterical fear. Many fled from the crowded cities to the country. But they often found all doors barred, for no one wished the disease brought into his house." This passage was taken from a chronicle relating to one of the most dreaded diseases of the Middle Ages. The panic was the result of a series of epidemics that plagued Europe in the fourteenth century. Its name—the Black Death. Millions died. Medical knowledge was hopelessly inadequate, and the causes of the plague were unknown.

The Church did what it had done for centuries before and has continued to do in the centuries since. It ministered to the victims asking no questions, blaming no one for having been afflicted. Religious and lay persons—priests, men, and women—took heroic risks, aware that contracting the disease meant almost certain death.

I am not comparing AIDS victims to either the victims of the Black Death or to those afflicted with leprosy. Such a comparison would be neither appropriate nor to the point. The point is that people in both time periods have had to deal with fear, panic, confusion, and endurance. The point is also that we are in what many health authorities call an epidemic, and we may have seen only the beginning of it.

93

Understandably, some people have reacted with fear bordering on panic. To blame them or to indict them is nonsensical. Most of them are less fearful for themselves than for their children and others they love. And why not? We always fear the unknown. We read whatever we can get our hands on about the origins and the nature of the disease—and a good bit has been written about AIDS. We listen to announcements from public health officials who try to reassure us. But many live with the nagging fear that these officials are either telling us information about which they are not sure or are not telling us all they know. Even the most trusting people find conflicting accounts in newspapers and periodicals about how the disease is transmitted. So there is honest and understandable fear.

In the meantime the victim suffer; their families and their children suffer. It is for this reason that the Greek Orthodox Church must do its part to try to help, regardless of the causes of the disease or how it has been contracted in any given case.

The Disease

This disease, which only began to be followed by the Center of Disease Control in Atlanta (CDC) in 1979, is caused by a virus labeled either HTLV-III (Human T-Cell Lymphotrophic Virus Type Three) or LAV (Lymphadenopathy Virus). The virus itself is not the real killer. However, it destroys the body's immune system, thus rendering the person prey to a variety of life-threatening illnesses. These illnesses are called "opportunistic infections" because they take the "opportunity" that an impaired immune system gives for the infection to enter the body and do its damage. The most common of these infections is a deadly form of pneumonia, which is found in 64 percent of the cases. *Kaposi's sarcoma,* a skin cancer, occurs in 24 percent of the cases. Once diagnosed, this disease moves with fearsome rapidity and has taken the lives of 55 percent of those diagnosed. The mean average time between the appearance of symptoms the disease's diagnosis is 3.5 months, and the mean between diagnosis and death has held at 5.6 months. Some persons who have AIDS die within days of diagnosis, while others have survived two to three years. (Statistics based on reports from 1985.)

Who is Affected

The catastrophic effects of AIDS primarily touches the lives of younger homosexual or bisexual males. Of the 20,760 cases cited, 47 percent are between 30 to 39 years old. Twenty-one percent are between 20 to 29 years old, and another 21 percent are between 40 to 49 years of age. In the face of the every-growing spread of this illness, it is necessary to know how the disease is transmitted and who is at risk for AIDS.

AIDS/HTLV disease is not spread because of who one is but because of what one does. It is spread by sexual acts that involve the exchange of body fluids. The virus can also be spread through the transfusion of untested blood (now all blood drawn in the United States is automatically tested) and blood products or the sharing of blood contaminated needles. An infected mother can pass the virus to her newborn child before or during birth. It is not the fact that persons are IV drug users that puts them at high risk for AIDS but that they share their needles with another after usage. It is not a man's homosexual orientation that puts him at risk for AIDS but the kind of intimate behavior that he might engage in.

The disease is also financially devastating. From the onset of symptoms to death, the disease costs about $139,000 per case. Few in this age group most susceptible to AIDS have the capital or insurance coverage to underwrite their medical treatment. Hospital specialists are aware that AIDS is not only killing people but is also killing hospitals.

The Stigma

It is important to mention a corollary to our discussion of those at high risk. This corollary is the "stigma factor." Grievous illness isolates the sufferer. The AIDS patient experiences this isolation in a heightened state due to the stigma that has been attached to this disease. A lack of understanding causes many people to feel that AIDS patients are a medical danger to them. In reality, people who have the flu are more of a danger to the AIDS patient than the patient is to them. Some attach a religious significance to the AIDS victim's diagnosis: "God is punishing you for your sexual orientation." Others, through ignorance, attach a moral judgement, thinking that this disease is associated with promiscuity, little realizing that it can be contracted from a single encounter.

The ignorance and judgments that stigmatize the AIDS patient then can be disastrous. Such ignorance has led to the untold suffering of children who have AIDS who are barred from classes and from association with their playmates. Over 1,700 cases of those living with a diagnosed person with AIDS have been studied, and in no case has the virus been transmitted through casual contact from the sufferer to the companion/caregiver. Nonetheless, due to widespread ignorance, many AIDS patients can tell horror stories of being shunned, outcast, and bereft of society.

A recently diagnosed AIDS victim stated, "I wish I could tell my boss I had lung cancer. It would be so much easier." Another person with AIDS rejoiced when his physician told him that along with his other infections, he now had lung cancer. He was almost elated and certainly relieved that now he could tell his mother that he was dying of a more respectable disease. He did not want her to suffer from his stigma.

Another factor of the AIDS stigma is that it is multidirectional; you need not have AIDS to suffer from it. Support groups exist for families and friends of people who have AIDS not only to help them cope with the death and dying of a child, friend, spouse, or brother but also to assist them in dealing with the stigma. The stigma surrounding AIDS has led some employers to terminate employees infected with HIV who were otherwise able to work. The AIDS stigma, with its accompanying hysteria, has led some people to evict AIDS victims who have to seek refuge on the street and public shelters. Many of them can tell the litany of "man's inhumanity to man."

An Orthodox Response

In the days of the early Church, the sick were always a special concern of the Christian community. Traditionally, when people fled to the countryside to avoid sickness, plagues, cholera, and leprosy, the Church—countless religious and lay persons—ministered to the sick and the dying in adherence to St. Iakovos' admonition in his Epistle—read during every sacrament of Holy Unction, "Is anyone among you sick? Let him bring the presbyters of the Church, and let them pray over him, anointing him with oil in the name of the Lord" (Catholic Epistle of Iakovos, 1:14). Many of the ascetic Fathers of the Church dedicated their lives to serving lepers and other sick persons, and many of them fell victim to the same diseases.

Today, the Christian community is called to witness to the presence of Christ in those suffering from Acquired Immune Deficiency Syndrome. Although the chances of catching AIDS are miniscule, the struggle against ignorance, superstition, and fear is the same as in the past. When the first federal government report on AIDS by the Center for Disease Control in Atlanta, Georgia, came out in June of 1981, very little was known about the disease. A few doctors had recognized a pattern of infectious diseases among homosexuals. After the first study, doctors from around the country began reporting similar cases. Most victims were homosexual men, although in Africa, where it is probably transmitted by prostitutes, it is just as common among heterosexuals.

Today, the most recent report tells us that intravenous drug users and blood transfusion recipients are also victims of this dreaded disease.

From statistical research, it is know that about 6,000 Americans have died of AIDS and that another 6,000 are known to have the disease. No one has as yet recovered from the disease.

In New York City, AIDS is now the leading cause of death among men between 25 and 44 years of age. Some experts believe that the number of AIDS patients will double by 1991. In addition, the Center for Disease Control believes that there are as many as 120,000 cases of AIDS-related complex, or A R C, which does not always develop into AIDS. Finally, some studies estimate that as many as one million Americans are symptomless carriers of the virus.

A few things about AIDS have become clear in the last four years. The disease is transmitted through the exchange of bodily fluids-primarily through sexual activity but also through the sharing of unsterilized hypodermic needles and through blood transfusions. Whether AIDS could be transmitted through saliva has as yet been undetermined, but it is considered unlikely. Testing procedures are now in place that will eliminate blood transfusions as a cause of AIDS. It is also noteworthy that no doctors or nurses treating AIDS victims have died of the disease. If the disease were easily caught, medical personnel would have been the first victims. No vaccine or cure is on the horizon, and much more private and government research is needed.

Recently, many clergymen of every denomination have contended that AIDS victims are being punished for their sins. This claim is not only an ignorant point of view, but it is also un-Orthodox. Although there is a relationship between sickness and man's sinful condition, sickness cannot be considered a punishment that man suffers for his personal sins. In the sacrament of Holy Unction at the prayer of anointing, the priest or bishop prays at the very end of the service, "O Holy Father, physician of souls and bodies, who didst send Thine only begotten Son, our Lord Jesus Christ, who heals every infirmity and delivers us from death: heal, also, Thy servants from the ills of the body and soul which do hinder them, and quicken them by the grace of Thy Christ." And in the Gospel of John 9:3, we read: "Jesus answered, 'His blindness has nothing to do with his sins or his parents' sins. He is blind so that God's power might be seen at work in him'." We must never stray from the true purpose of Christianity! We must see in the AIDS victim a brother or sister in Christ who deserves our love and our help. To use the gospel or the Church to avoid our obligation to an AIDS victim is to shun Christ Himself.

Christian hospitals, Orthodox physicians, chaplains, doctors, nurses, and other medical personnel have a special responsibility for the care of AIDS victims. It is, however, clear that the government is going to have to take a greater role in supporting research of this disease and caring for its victims. But while love and compassion are offered to those stricken by AIDS, no one should falsely promise solutions that would lead people to doubt that monogamy and self-control not only make moral sense but medical sense as well. We must also take a very close look at the consequences of immorality in a secular humanistic society.

Interdisciplinary Report on AIDS

Special Committee

Because of of concerns that Orthodox Christians have expressed about the impact that the disease AIDS has had upon their lives, and because of questions regarding the transmission of HIV, the Orthodox Christian Association of Medicine, Psychology and Religion (O.C.A.M.P.R.) convened a forum of leaders in these fields. This forum addressed specific questions raised by Church leaders in an effort to offer an interdisciplinary perspective relative to the faith and AIDS. Those questions are as follows:

1. Should there be an alteration in the administration Holy Communion to guard against contamination or in response to the fear of HIV?

2. Should people wanting to marry be tested for HIV?

3. What kind of behavior ought to be recommended in order to avoid the spread of AIDS?

4. How do we counsel people to respond to AIDS patients and to the fear of the spread of this disease?

This report has been prepared to facilitate an understanding about AIDS for Orthodox Christians. It is not intended as a position paper as such but works to identify several points of view raised in the religious and scientific communities. This report is submitted with the hope that as the Church responds to the subject of

AIDS, pastoral sensitivity will address the following concerns:

1.   Should the administration of Holy Communion be altered from the *lavida* and chalice to guard against contamination or in response to the fear of HIV?

    A.   Risk of transmission of HIV and Holy Communion

    The transmission of AIDS by means of the chalice used in Holy Communion seems to be highly unlikely, given the concentration of HIV necessary for infection and the fragility of the virus outside of the body. Current medical information, however, does not rule out transmission by way of the chalice.

    AIDS has polarized some members within the Church Body about the current practice of administering Holy Communion because of the potential contamination of HIV during Holy Communion. On the one hand, Holy Communion is, for Orthodox Christians, the Body and Blood of Christ and therefore the vehicle for life, not death. On the other hand, the specific question raised by the disease of AIDS is whether the HIV virus, or germs generally, can be transmitted when one receives Holy Communion. Therefore, concern about AIDS has raised a wider question about the transmission of germs generally via the current medium for receiving the Communion.

    Distinctions need to be drawn in this discussion. As Faithful Orthodox Christians affirm the reality of Jesus Christ in Holy Communion. At the same time it is noted that the purpose of Holy Communion is not to destroy destructive viruses, but to act as a means to healing according to one's faith and to the Grace of God. Therefore, one cannot be certain what impact the HIV or other germs or viruses might have in Holy Communion or if or how Holy Communion neutralizes them.

    For sometime this dilemma has made receiving Holy Communion a test to evaluate one's spiritual and possibly physical well-being. Holy Communion should not be perceived as a test to prove one's worthiness to God or to demonstrate something about his or her relationship with Him. As the current practice for the administration of receiving Holy Communion has created such a challenge for some of the members of the Church Body, this subject invites a pastoral response.

    B.   Pastoral concerns regarding altering the form of administration of Holy Communion

    Church history indicates Holy Communion has been administered in various ways. Currently, there is no agreement about the need nor a consensus about how to alter Holy Communion. But should there be a change Church members should not view it as either inherently "good" or "bad." Change that is consistent with the Orthodox Tradition is certainly conceivable within the Church. Therefore, as this matter is considered, change should not evolve as a response to fear but as a legitimate expression of pastoral sensitivity.

2. Should people wanting to marry be tested for HIV?

As a general rule, if one has doubt whether or not he or she has been exposed to HIV, it is advisable for that person to be tested for HIV antibodies. It is important for potential spouses to know whether they are carriers of HIV or if they are at risk of contracting AIDS after marriage. In the interest of facilitating and supporting a solid base for a prospective marriage in these days, AIDS testing before marriage would probably be reassuring to a couple and would possibly be helpful. Therefore, it is recommended.

At the same time, it should be noted that test results have various limitations. The Church should be supportive and encourage such practices, but it should not be involved in the technical, procedural or legal aspects or requirements for such testing before marriage.

3. What kind of behavior ought to be recommended in order to avoid the spread of AIDS?

First, Church members should be informed about the disease and its spread. Behaviors that are in accordance with the faith (for example, morality as opposed to promiscuity, prostitution, and drug abuse) and that avoid routes for the spread of the disease dangers (for example, sharing needles) need to be encouraged. The scientific community recommends monogamous behavior to avoid or at least to decrease the spread of AIDS.

Second, the Church supports sex education that encourages dating in which people are conscious of their behavior, or the rules of chastity, and in which "pre-intimate" partners agree to testing for HIV antibodies. Religious education that addresses these concerns should guide the faithful toward lifetime, monogamous relationships based upon trust, love and fidelity.

4. How do you counsel people to respond to AIDS patients and to the fear of the spread of this disease?

The faithful should be educated as to how HIV is contracted. Studies of thousands of AIDS patients who have non-sexual, close and familial contacts strongly support the belief that HIV does not spread via close personal contact. As people are educated and feel less at risk by interaction with AIDS patients, social attitudes will improve.

Compassion of the faithful for persons with AIDS and their families needs to be encouraged. The Church must work actively against prejudice and fear through its spiritual resources of Christian hope, faith and love and through specific educational efforts.

Sex education concerning one's faith generally should be part of religious programming. Subjects such as multiple sexual partners, sexual expression, monogamy and abstinence, and drug use and abuse, need to be addressed openly, directly and in the Tradition of the faith. Additionally, Orthodox people should be taught how to treat persons affected by AIDS with an emphasis on love, compassion and instruction on how to deal with those facing death.

The subject of AIDS is one of the most critical problems of this century. The Church has a responsibility to provide leadership, direction and counsel regarding various aspects of this issue and to draw upon resourcefulness of the Body of Believers with the guidance of Jesus Christ in its response.

AIDS Committee

Dr. George Canellos - Professor of Medicine, Harvard Medical School; Medical Director, Dana Farber Cancer Institute

Dr. John T. Chirban (Chairman) - Professor of Psychology and Religion, Hellenic College; Associate in Human Development, Harvard University

Rev. Dr. Stanley S. Harakas - Professor of Orthodox Theology and Christian Ethics, Holy Cross School of Theology

Dr. Matina S. Horner - President, Radcliffe College; Associate Professor of Psychology, Harvard University

Rev. George Johnson - Pastor, Johnstown, Pennsylvania, Orthodox Church in America

Dr. Nikos Kakaviatos - Cardiologist; President, Washington, D.C. District O.C.A.M.P.R.

His Grace Bishop Methodios of Boston, Greek Orthodox Archdiocese

Mr. George Morelli - Clinical Psychologist and Assistant Pastor of the Antiochian Orthodox Church of Brooklyn, New York

Dr. Anthony Parris - Dermatologist; Chairman, O.C.A.M.P.R. Division of Medicine

Dr. George Pazin - Infectious Disease Specialist, Associate Professor of Medicine, University of Pittsburgh School of Medicine

Mr. Peter Poulos - Director of Clinical Pastoral Education, The Methodist Hospital, Brooklyn, New York

Rev. Dr. Theodore Stylianopoulos - Professor of New Testament and Orthodox Spirituality, Holy Cross School of Theology

Experiences in Cancer: Bridging the Gap Between Patients and Professionals

Georgia Photopulos

Cancer does not attack the body alone! No matter how, when or where cancer enters a person's life, it brings with it a sense of fear and delivers a devastating blow to the patient and to the entire family as well. The diagnosis of the disease, along with its medical procedures, surgical scars, and therapeutic side-effects, can impose a heavy burden not only on the patient but on family and, frequently, friends and co-workers, as it disrupts their life style, creates uncertainty about the future, and causes financial upheaval.

Because of the fear, anxiety, and distress cancer brings with it, it is not simply an enemy of the body but an enemy of the psyche as well. It attacks the emotions as it attacks the tissues. Often the damage to the patient's emotional well-being is more serious than the damage to his or her body. Those patients whose emotional hurt can be more acute than their physical pain often suffer unbearable feelings of anger, depression, and humiliation—feelings that can ultimately result in their isolation from relatives, friends, and other patients. Patients are sorely in need of understanding, empathy, and concern about their very real problems. They need genuine help in learning to cope with and find solutions to problems already experienced by others who have preceded them in the struggle with cancer.

Patients often have questions that are not always answered by their doctors and other medical personnel: fears that are not shared with their families and not allayed by their ministers; problems that are not solved because there is too little help

105

available and because patients too frequently mask their true needs. Patients who do not have this interpersonal communication can often find themselves at the point of no return. But with an awareness of human strengths and weaknesses, patients and professionals alike can develop a flow of understanding that is mutually beneficial and *not* mutually exclusive.

To put it another way, *no one* knows more about how it feels to have cancer than a cancer patient. It is hard to face. The word alone strikes terror in everyone's hearts. An ever-present Sword of Damocles hangs over the cancer patient's head, and newly imposed disciplines, an altered way of life, and perhaps a body that is altered as well, are constant reminders of his or her frailty and mortality. These fears and apprehensions do not grow smaller as the years go by. Instead, the battle to survive becomes increasingly more difficult. No magic potion blots out these thoughts when they surface, and the going can get rough. But in order to survive, one must work through these fears by exploring his or her own value system and develop an applicable source of determination and a sense of purpose to see him or herself through.

I was 34 years old when cancer and I discovered we had each other. By the grace of God and with the help of medical science, I am alive—but I have fought hard to stay alive. I have drawn on every ounce of energy at my command to wage this battle. I have undergone many radical surgical procedures, which includes two mastectomies and a hysterectomy; I have received 120 treatments of radiation therapy; I have undergone nuclear scans and countless medical procedures, exams, and lab tests—all of which become a routine way of life for most cancer patients. In destroying the disease that invaded my body, medical science has also destroyed other vital systems within my body—damage that will be with me forever. Despite handicaps and complications, however, I feel fortunate that I have resumed a creative, meaningful life.

I received the initial diagnosis of cancer on my tenth wedding anniversary in 1968 and when my children Jim and Kerry were 5 and 2 years old. My prognosis was poor, and my pain was great. My husband, Bud, and I discovered first-hand that the pain of a loved one becomes the pain of the other; the hurt of a loved one is the hurt of the other. For cancer is not an illness that one suffers through alone. It involves one's family, friends, and colleagues who, to one degree or another, share the illness with the patient.

Although these stressful years have brought pain, fear, uncertainty, and anguish, they have also brought hope and a sense of victory. I have learned that there are only two ways of coping with cancer: either you fight it and give yourself a chance to live or you surrender to it. I decided to fight, and in so doing, I discovered that fear was my biggest enemy. Fearing cancer is worse than having it. Fear is what makes a person delay seeking treatment. Fear cripples one's ability to deal with it; and fear, ultimately, can be fatal.

No one has ever been cured of cancer by ignoring it! I am alive today because I faced it directly and did what had to be done. Yet, accepting the terrible truth is just part of the struggle. For when a person's strength is at its lowest ebb, one is called on to marshall all his or her resources—physical and emotional—to put up the fight of one's life.

Why, I wondered, should anyone face it alone? The answer was as obvious as the question: *One shouldn't*. There is no more hopeless a feeling than that of being totally alone in a crisis. A person needs more than his or her doctor when fighting cancer; he or she needs someone to lean on, someone to talk to, someone who will listen, someone who cares and understands—someone who has not only walked in his or her shoes, but *who is still around leaving footprints!* To shed light on these issues, I will share some of my experiences and thoughts.

Because I decided to fight my cancer, I had no choice but to go on a wild roller coaster ride, dragging my husband and two children along with me. Because Jim and Kerry where young and vulnerable and because cancer is such an *unknown*, it was imperative that we dealt honestly with the situation, and yet we tried to provide a sense of normalcy at home. Things were happening so fast, though, that my every homecoming was met with mixed emotions. The joy and relief felt by all were overshadowed by the anticipation of returning to the hospital for more surgery and more treatments. Adversity hovered over us like an ominous cloud. Our medical expenses were devastating, and it was difficult for us to manage without many of the things that would have enabled us to accommodate the problems caused by my illness. For example, we did not have household help or mothers to help with the children and to drive them to school lessons and other activities; my husband did not have the kind of job where he could take off when he needed to. As an ABC television *Network News* reporter, major stories—such as civil rights marches, riots, plane crashes, assassinations, the Olympic, and so forth—would unfold and he would be called into work. He would race from a late-breaking story to see me in the hospital, and then hurry home to be with the children. These circumstances tore us apart emotionally because we drew our strength from each other, but because changing jobs meant losing my hospitalization coverage, we tried to cherish the time we did have together.

My mother, who is extremely close to me, felt especially guilty about cancer. She was not only devastated by my illness, but because cancer was predominant on her side of the family, she felt responsible. Her grief was so acute that it was impossible for her to help us. So the children were better off staying with close friends who could follow more normal routines. Shortly before I got sick, my dad and grandmother had died and my mother had not had time to grieve for those losses. My husband and I discussed this and realized that if my mother and I were to preserve our special relationship, it was best that she not make her home with us. I needed to devote my energies to fighting my illness and, frankly, my mom pulled me down emotionally. She lived with her brother, a retired priest, in Oklahoma, where she felt needed. In the meantime, I did not have her come to me when I was hospitalized but only when I was home, to be my companion rather than my care-giver. My mother-in-law, who was also widowed by cancer and lives near us, is great during adversity, even though I know she shares my pain almost as much as my own mothers does.

Luckily, we have been blessed with many friends who helped us immensely. They have helped with the children, have driven me to doctor appointments, have gotten groceries, cooked, and helped with housework. But one's relationship with friends has drawbacks, too. Friends have sometimes been reluctant to call us be-cause they are busy or feel that they are disturbing us if I have just come home from the hospital. We, in turn, have been hesitant to call them; because they have helped so often over the years, we fear they might mistake a social call as another plea for help. So there is an awkward strain on friendships, and cancer scores an-other point. Friends are often frustrated and bewildered and with good reason. They are grateful that they are not the patient, all the while truly empathizing with the one who is, that they experience difficulty in dealing with their emotions. It is easier for them to pull away to deal with their own emotions so when the patient most needs support, the friend is least capable of providing it. Also, the disparity between their lives and ours leads to awkwardness. They seem financially stable, purchasing homes, furniture, vacations, and so forth, while ours seems to be going in reverse from all the medical bills.

It is terribly difficult for me to ask for help, because I have always been a giver. Now, for over 7,000 days, I have often been forced into the role of a taker, so I continually push myself harder to accomplish more. I am trying to hang on to my dignity and independence.

The enormity of this struggle and the emotional, financial, and physical bur-dens cancer has imposed on my loved ones has caused me to suffer a profound sense of guilt. To compensate for this intrusion in our lives, I have tried to be all things to all people—particularly to those afflicted with illness—to honor my early commitment to God. But in return, every new blessing I have experienced out-weighs the last one. I am sure that this is because my faith in God has never wa-vered. In fact, after surgery I was able to rebound in a way that even overwhelmed me.

In February, 1984, I underwent brain surgery. Miraculously, the huge arach-noid cyst at the base of the brain was benign. A permanent shunt was placed in my brain to drain fluid into my spinal column. I recuperated remarkably well, eager to be in charge of myself again and looking forward to going home to my family.

When persons have been cancer patients as as long as I have, they find them-selves bargaining for good news, but they usually do not get it. Nine days after that surgery, the bad news came. My pain was enormous—worse than any I had ever had. The shunt in my brain had become infected, and I had developed meningitis. I was paralyzed and was hooked into a battery of intravenous medication that made me feel like I was being kept prisoner in my bed. My speech became so slurred that it was difficult to understand. I was bewildered by this sudden development. One moment I was well on my way to recovery, and the next I was more ill than ever before and had to fight harder than ever to get well. In fact, more brain surgery was being considered to replace the infected shunt.

My constant faith in God has sustained me through every adversity and aided my recuperation. I do not know if optimism is a hereditary trait or develops later in life, but I surely consider it my strongest asset. My doctors have repeatedly told me that this attitude has helped me greatly in fighting cancer and that if anyone could survive *brain surgery* with a smile, that someone was me! I know I have been lucky and the pain has been worth it. I have had twenty operations, and I am practically good as new! What amazes me in particular is that I do not panic before these terrifying surgeries. I pray for *peace of mind*, and I seem to have it. I am able to see things clearly and "soar" above the situation as if it were happening to someone else. Then I am able meditate on my alternatives between life and death and not fall apart. I do not drink or need sedatives or tranquilizers and am fully in control. I am sure it is by Divine Grace that I have the peace I pray for.

Several months ago, I had another Magnetic Resonance Imaging Scan (MRI). If the enormous motor coordination problems I earlier experienced had indeed been eliminated by the surgery and shunt implant, then I could have fearlessly resumed my activities, including driving on icy, snowy roads. To my astonishment, the *after* scans were identical to the ones *before*—the cyst was there.

My neurosurgeons have determined that it has probably been there many years—maybe not as large as it is now or perhaps maybe not causing the pressures it conceivably should or the brain damage that would be expected from a growth of this size, but they feel it is untreatable and inoperable. Realistically, I am aware of the possibly serious consequences of this cyst. But I feel that my attitude is more important than the facts revealed by the scanner. I may not be able to alter the situation, but I can exercise control over how I accept and deal with it. That is why I emphasize that it is essential that hope never be taken away from the patient.

When cancer becomes a threat to the functioning of a family system, re-evaluation of old rules, changes in priorities, and new flexibility become necessary. When a family is waiting in the surgical lounge,they are stalked by fear. When the doctor says it doesn't look good, implying that cancer has been found, many families never move beyond this point in time—no matter how successful the outcome may be. Their world has been shattered.

Ethnic groups pose a special problem in dealing with this concern. I have found that women from many ethnic backgrounds are unfamiliar with most medical terms and are reluctant to accept the idea of preventive medicine. They are unaware of the value of breast self-examination and a Pap smear and are reluctant to be examined by a doctor. Many bring with them the attitudes of their mother countries, and if those attitudes include feminine modesty, they prevent these women from seeking medical care. Many of these same women have never been assisted by a doctor, even during childbirth—they have had mid-wives. Those who do seek a doctor generally select one whom they know is socially active in their community, but who may not be equipped to detect, diagnose, or treat cancer. Consequently, these patients rarely survive.

While everyone has good days and bad days, cancer patients seem to chalk up more bad ones. This claim does not mean that I am pessimistic, hostile, or irrational; it means we are terrified by a life-threatening illness, and we need support and understanding. It is important to recognize that a patient's negative moods are temporary and *not* an attack on loved ones or those around him. A family struggling with cancer can be under such extreme psychological pressure that it builds to the danger point. A patient is deeply loved but has been ill for a very long time. Relatives and friends can barely hide flashes of resentment at the burden of caring for or assisting the patient, especially when the patient is constantly cranky. One member of the family might be furious because a brother, sister, or child is not doing everything possible to help. This strain is magnified even more when some family members live a distance away and cannot help out the people responsible for the day-to-day care-giving.

While the patient's suffering is easily recognized, that of his family is not. But everyone is hurting—patient, spouse, children, parents—and they cannot always see each other's pain. The family suffers along with the patient, yet does not get the same kind of support. They try to follow their daily routine—work, school, laundry, shopping, cooking. They fight traffic to visit the patient in the hospital and keep friends and relatives updated. It is a hassle for a week, and if the patient is hospitalized for five or six, the family can easily run itself into a state of exhaustion, trying to keep up with a frantic pace. They need a break. They need time to rest—to replenish their emotional reserves—but they do not get it. And chances are, when the patient leaves the hospital, his homecoming is not necessarily met with overwhelming enthusiasm, particularly if he needs continuing care at home. Managing pain and distress, providing special meals and medication, changing beds and bandages—the kind of care routinely provided in the hospital—cannot be duplicated easily at home. Consequently, the patient may feel that his family is just not sympathetic or trying hard enough. The family, now the full-time caregivers, may not be making those daily trips to the hospital, but the demands on their time and energy are at an all-time high.

When the patient is a child, the other children at home are disrupted emotionally and physically. They see less of their parents, whose attention is primarily focused on the child who is ill, and the others feel pushed out of their lives. They do not know how to verbalize their feelings, so they act them out by being cranky and rebellious.

Because the family's strain is not always visible, it is important that someone trusted by the patient explain when negative feelings surface within the family that it does not indicate a lack of love or concern. The patient needs this assurance. At the same time, the family needs some understanding of its own.

I have never believed that God does anything to us as a punishment, but it was not until I realized my own need for contact with other patients outside my family and friends that I sensed what I should do and set about doing it. My physical needs and questions were responded to by physicians, but no one wanted to respond to my anxieties and fears. As my disease progressed and the course of my treatments was extended, I had many more encounters with patients. A remarkably strong feeling of identity and fellowship emerged from that contact.

However, for decades patients were neither considered nor consulted by health care professionals to determine what those feelings might be. An admission of fear resulted in a referral to a psychiatrist. Anticipating this, the patient would mask his true feelings from even his primary physician. Clearly there was a need for a middle man between the surgeon's table and the psychiatrist's couch. In frequent lectures and during television interviews, I addressed the issues that troubled patients. The frank response from throughout the nation was overwhelming. They, too, knew where to go to resolve their *medical* questions, but their *emotional* needs were not being met.

The discovery that nothing existed in the way of psycho-social support for patients in 1969 provided the stimulus for me to develop a program through which successfully-adjusted patients could help one another through rough times. The American Cancer Society provided a small grant and asked me to research and develop my idea for such a hot-line that would meet the non-physical needs of cancer patients. The service became a reality and began operating throughout the Chicago area in June of 1973. Cancer Cal-Pac, or People Against Cancer, was the first of its kind and was widely acclaimed across the nation for fulfilling a previously untapped area of care. This unique service provides an emotional support hot-line available on a 24-hour basis and is manned by volunteer patients who have adapted to their diagnosis of cancer. It has served as the prototype for all cancer-related self-help programs in existence today. Since its inception, thousands of people from all walks of life have called us. They have shared their innermost fears and hopes. They seek understanding and a sense of direction from other patients who have had similar experiences.

While the 1970s became an unparalleled decade of discoveries in treatment modalities, research, and education, two very significant benefits resulting from these breakthroughs was the increase in survival of many more cancer patients and an upgraded quality of life for cancer patients. Because of their past successes in living with cancer and their willingness to assist others in the struggle for life, these recovered patients have formed the nucleus of emotional rehabilitation programs springing up today.

Seven years ago, it was necessary to sell the home we loved and had lived in for seventeen years. Doctors had warned us that my health could not tolerate three flights of stairs and no air-conditioning. We felt that the close proximity to a Greek Orthodox Church and the public school across the street made our house perfect for a young Greek family who did not have a car but who had children. Several Greek families responded immediately to the ad, but when they saw photos of my family and me, it killed their interest. Their realtors called to tell us that because of the superstition regarding cancer, none of the buyers felt comfortable buying a home that a cancer patient had previously occupied.

These kinds of cruel comments and superstitions are exactly why many people isolate themselves when cancer is diagnosed. But when they have someone to share these things with, they can be put into their proper prospective. We receive calls from young children wanting to know how to help a parent who has cancer— from children who feel that somehow they may have caused their parent's cancer. Some calls from families say that they care very deeply for the patient but they simply cannot handle the strain any more and ask where can they turn to for help. Some friends ask me, "How do you listen? How can I convey that I understand even though I do not have cancer?" We also get agonizing calls from patients asking, "What do you *do*—what *can* you do—on the days when you just don't feel like living?" They are not contemplating suicide; they are just trying to find a way to survive another painful day that cannot be distinguished from the previous one. We often hear, "I can cope with my cancer, but I literally scream when I look into a mirror and see that I've lost my hair. For me a wig is a necessity, not a luxury. Tell me where to get one."

And, on a lighter vein: A gentleman called an asked whether I agreed that the best way to communicate with a patient was to be direct? I said I thought so in most instances. He said, "Good, because my 52-year-old bachelor cousin is dying from cancer. The doctor says he only has several weeks to live, and it would be nice if he could spend these days at home with family. My wife and I can invite him to stay at our house since he's alone, but first we want to know who he's leaving his money to. If he's gonna leave it to someone else, then the missus and I aren't gonna waste our time caring for him. We feel that whoever gets the money should also take care of him. When you say communicate, do you mean I should come right out and ask him about the money?" I was aghast and said this was definitely *not* what I meant by communicating.

Some people seem to think cancer diminishes mental ability. Well, it does not. When we struggle with physical pain and emotional anguish, it is easy for others to assume that our stress is making us go crazy. So patients hurt when others tell them what to do or treat them as if they were stupid.

Another prevalent myth is that cancer is contagious. It is *not*; people can be cruel by implying that it is. I have even been asked if my cancer might be transmitted to someone else while receiving Holy Communion.

Prior to his illness, a cancer patient and his wife played cards regularly with a group of neighbors. After his recuperation, he assumed things would continue as before. But he was wrong. At the next game, his host and hostess made their feelings apparent by serving him with a paper plate and plastic spoons, while all the others used china and silverware.

The best thing that caregivers can do for cancer patients is make the climate as comfortable as possible; allow the patient to maintain his dignity; define what help is available; and then if the patient chooses to see a psychiatrist or psychologist, he will feel that he helped in that decision, rather than thinking he has been forced into it because his reaction or response to his illness is such an abnormal one.

Sometimes a spouse who appears to be very supportive is merely performing. She or he can be actually uncaring, unsupportive, and even cruel to the patient, but if a doctor tells the patient about how fortunate she or he is to have such a caring spouse, he or she feels guilty. Doctors should learn to ask the patient how he or she feels his or her spouse has responded to crises in the past, and how he or she will respond now.

It is important to remember that the majority of people who find out that they have cancer have entered the hospital with an undiagnosed ailment or a suspicion of cancer and have submitted to a battery of tests. If surgery is indicated, it is often performed by their family doctor or an associate of his. Thus, if cancer is detected following surgery, people often choose to stay at their local hospital for a variety of reasons—fear of alienating the physician, ignorance, denial, or the lack of realization that better care exists elsewhere. So a woman who had a cancerous breast removed may share a room with someone who may have had an emergency appendectomy, cosmetic, or other elective surgery.

If the health care delivery team does not deal appropriately with the patient who has received a diagnosis of cancer, the patient masks his or her fears and tears so he or she won't depress or annoy her roommate. Outwardly, everything looks great, and the family is also relieved that they do not have to deal openly with the enormous new problems cancer has brought to them and their loved one.

Because being a cancer patient becomes a lifelong process for many, cancer patients must draw a distinction between coping with life's problems and coping with cancer. A recent National Cancer Institute publication stresses, "Coping is defined simply as adaptation under difficult circumstances, and includes any strategy used by cancer patients, their family members, and caregivers to deal with the psychological and physical threats imposed by cancer." They conclude that "most cancer patients are essentially stable people who are dealing with a series of very difficult situations." Through my extensive involvement with literally thousands of patients and families, it has became evident to me that these people have psychosocial concerns that they would *willingly* share if they felt they would be understood, and that those who *do* have coping strengths do not realize how valuable these strengths are when they are *not* afforded the opportunity to communicate with others faced with similar problems. Attempted psycho-social questioning by trained interviewers and members of the caregiving team has not always met with success because patient response has not proven to be as candid as had been hoped for. For example:

- Can a patient tell his physician, who has "life and death" power over him, that he is *not* providing the emotional support he urgently needs?

- Can a patient who shares his unmet needs or fears with the caregiving team be certain that the information will be used to help him—and not as "gossip"?

- Can a patient criticize the services that he receives from the caregiving team, regardless of how ineffective the support may be, and not be ignored later because he or she was considered a complainer?

- Must a patient who quickly learns that "good behavior gets rewarded" by the caregiving team need to fear neglect or abandonment if his less-than-cooperative disposition and anger at the disease are allowed to surface around those directly responsible for his needs?

What is needed is a systematic method of establishing psychological and social dimensions of coping strategies and unmet needs for cancer patients that includes many cancer patients from many backgrounds with many types of cancer. There should be a vehicle for allowing patients to voice their perceptions of their overall treatment by the various health disciplines. This information could provide effective methods of eliminating frustration and *burn out* by professional caregives who treat cancer patients. Results from this kind of study would provide the data necessary to create a flow of understanding and communication between patients and their caregivers. By understanding each other's strengths and weaknesses, a two-way avenue of communication can eliminate what has heretofore been two mutually exclusive ones.

In the meantime, I know that I have kept my promise to God and have opened many doors. I am firmly convinced that I have done what He wanted me to do. I have also learned that hope is something to live for, that fear can be less fearsome, that anguish can be made easier to bear, and that understanding is attainable.

Part Five

Miracles and Technology

Miracles: A Medical Perspective

Theoharis C. Theoharides

The word *miracle—ναυμα* in Greek—obviously denotes something that generates wonder. The term was used by Homer and Hesiod in various settings. The English word derives from Latin and denotes the same thing as the Greek but is primarily an event that occurs in human affairs for which we really have no explanation, causing us to attribute it to a divine or supernatural intervention. Greek tragedies often ended by what was called divine intervention, or a *πο μηχανης νεος*. Over the years, there have been numerous attempts to explain the miraculous in medical or realistic terms,[1] an attempt that culminated in the "Psychiatric Study of Jesus."[2]

The world around us is clearly one of the best examples of a miracle, and our attempt to understand it comprises a series of small miracles in their own right. Our ability to try to explain the world around us clearly derives from our analytical powers, which depend on the neurons—the specialized cells that make up our brain. These neurons have the theoretical ability to make as many connections in a lifetime as there are molecules in the universe, a power that is really stupefying and constitutes, at least in my mind, a miracle in and of itself.

---

[1]E. Le Bec, *Medical Proof of the Miraculous: A Clinical Study.* Harding and Moore, Ltd: London, 1922, pp. 1-198.

[2]Albert Schweitzer, *The Psychiatric Study of Jesus.* The Beacon Press: Boston, 1948.

The fight between the powers of good evil and is a notion that has been carried through the centuries and has colored the study and possible understanding of miracles. The curing of the possessed by Christ in one of the best ways of depicting how a miracle may occur. This miracle, as depicted on a sixteenth century icon from Mount Athos, shows something concrete in the sense that our Lord could expel a demon from an epileptic patient with words and a gesture. At the extreme opposite of this simple gesture is the scientific unpredictability of the universe. When young Einstein developed the theory of relativity, he proclaimed that the beauty of the world around us clearly could not be explained by our very poor ability to predict where some atoms might jump from one place to another.[3] It is this inability to understand a very complex and miraculous universe that makes us so skeptical about a simple gesture from our Lord being able to cure a complicated clinical entity such as epilepsy.

This detail of the icon stresses the Lord's attempt to make both verbal and physical contact with the patient. This can be considered one of the first attempts to indicate somehow that there is *human contact* or *communication* in such phenomena that would otherwise be called miraculous. In another sixteenth century icon from Mount Athos, one observes the dialogue between Ioannis the Theologos and Cynops, the leader of the demons. During this presentation, a number of possessed people are actually cured through a *dialogue*; the miraculous cure is therefore endowed with some human qualities, such as the power of speech, which is so characteristic of present-day psychotherapy.

In a scientific paper entitled "Ticket to Heaven," the authors examined some communities in ancient Ethiopia.[4] These communities drew to them people considered outcasts of society. These individuals' characteristics exhibited a lack of ability to conform to society's norms. Today, such characteristics would be indications of severe psychiatric disease, and these individuals would probably be institutionalized. Instead, they were operating fairly efficiently within the context of that mini-society. One may call this phenomenon a miracle of love, which brings us to what I consider the ultimate miracle: the fact that God embraced us all with such love that He assumed human nature and was sacrificed for us. This love of His, then, crowned by His resurrection, is the most miraculous event known. Love—and love for God—could therefore be a very powerful source in our attempt to explain miracles. How could such love possibly allow us to have a vision of the miraculous? A recent television advertisement may help explain this phenomenon. It shows a glass filled with water to the mid-point. The commentator says, "Some consider this glass half empty, and some consider it half full; however, one could see it as the way to permit a rosebud placed in the water to blossom."

How a miraculous process works may be illustrated by using the example of

---

[3]"Conservative Einstein." *New York Times*, May 4, 1935.
[4]R. Giel. "Ticket to Heaven: Psychiatric Illness in a Religious Community in Ethiopia." *Social Science & Medicine*, 8:549-556, 1974.

dermatography, which has been used over the centuries as proof of the miraculous. In this phenomenon, the skin of certain individuals shows letters when pressed. When a population of cells in the skin called mast cells, which are full of granules, are stimulated, they undergo an explosive release of their contents.[5] It was not until the early 1950s that the release of at least one molecule, histamine, from such cells could clearly explain the swelling of the skin that resulted in a welt-like appearance of letters where pressed.

The Greeks first thought that the life force resided in the site of the diaphragm (φρην). Interestingly, in Biblical Greek this term is retained in the word αφρων, which denotes someone foolish; it was later used in the term *phrenology*, the "science" of studying behavior by examining the shape of the skull. Today, we try to understand the brain by focusing on certain specific areas and how distinct molecules bind to them. Such molecules can influence the brain in very different ways—for example, to create or alleviate pain or to change mood.

Because our brain communicates with most organs in the body, it can drastically alter the physiology of the rest of the body. Central effects in the brain could therefore possibly explain such disparate findings as might occur in what we would otherwise call miraculous cures. Some examples may help illustrate this point: Migraine headaches are possibly the most excruciating type of headache and are even today still associated with another condition, epilepsy. It is presently believed that at the beginning of a migraine some major veins going to the brain first constrict and then dilate. It is during the first phase of constriction that retinal vessels constrict and lead to a pattern of visual hallucinations—in other words, flashing lights and honeycomb shapes—that has given rise to the belief that such individuals may indeed be possessed. It is during the second dilation phase that patients feel the throbbing pain. Mast cell mediators are thought to play a major role in the pathophysiology of these events.[6] We can, therefore, see how characteristics that can clearly be explained in biological terms have led to what has otherwise been called possession and how the cure for such individuals might have been called miraculous.

Migraine patients are presently treated by substances called ergot alkaloids.[7] It is interesting to note that these substances derive from a fungus growing on wet rye, the ingestion of which could lead to a condition termed *convulsive ergotism*, which is characterized by hallucinations. It was these substances that gave rise to the massive hysteria of young women in the sixteenth century in Salem,

---

[5]T. C. Theoharides, "Mast Cells and Precursor Protein Molecules," *Perp. Biol. Med.* 24:499-502, 1981.

[6]T. C. Theoharides, "Mast Cells and Migraines," *Perp. Biol. Med.* 26:672-675, 1983.

[7]L. Lasagna, "Pain and Its Management," *Hospital Practice* 21:92C-92X, 1986.

Massachusetts.[8] Unfortunately, the psychologists of the time—the physicians and the priests—considered these young women to be witches and condemned them to the torch.[9] Indeed, it is a miracle to me how we can be so blinded by our assumptions that we understand human nature.

In the case of epilepsy, it is known that a small area in the brain could become epileptongenic. Such areas generate electrical activity that can cause the symptoms of epileptic seizures. We now know that our brain cells show what is called plasticity: they have the ability to change their characteristics almost entirely and have therefore the innate ability to change so that one may, in principle, be able to either alter or bypass the epileptic site altogether. We still have no idea how such an event happens, but the fact that we do not understand something today and call it miraculous does not mean that it will not someday have an explanation that we can all understand scientifically. The same holds true for mental illness.[10]

Our age has been defined as the age of anxiety.[11] We have powerful drugs to tamper with such conditions; however, the most common of these classes of drugs, the benzodiazepines causes depression if used in high doses. Indeed, practically all major classes of drugs have depression as a major side effect. In a sense, some of the major conditions that afflict the human race medically seem to derive from what we do to ourselves and to the environment; recognizing and trying to correct such factors as removing a medication that might have caused depression may at times be construed as constituting a miraculous cure.

Our efforts to understand nature should also demonstrate humility about what we know and what we can master. In a seventeenth century icon from Crete, St. Anthony is depicted holding a scroll that reads: "He who is humble can humble the demons." Humility is a lesson appropriate to the modern medical scientist as well. For instance, aspirin has been called the wonder drug of the twentieth century. Yet, it was used by Hippocrates around 300 B.C. when he asked pregnant women to chew on bitter willow leaves to ease the pains of childbirth. It was not until 1887 that the German firm Bayer synthesized acetyl salicylic acid by extracting salisylic acid (the active ingredient in aspirin) from bitter willow leaves.[12] The recognition, therefore, of what took more than 3,000 years or so to understand should indicate that it may take another 3,000 years before we understand processes we today call miracles.

---

[8]M. K. Matossian, "Ergot and the Salem Witchcraft Affair," *American Science* 70:355-357, 1982.

[9]P. J. Swales, "A Fascination with Witches," *The Sciences* 22:21-25, 1982.

[10]J. Miller, "The Myth of Mental Illness," *The Sciences* 23:22-30, 1983.

[11]M. Clark, *et al.*, "Drugs for the Mind," *Newsweek*, November 12:98-104, 1979.

[12]M. Clark and M. Hager, "An Old Drug's New Miracles," *Newsweek*, May 10:91-92, 1982.

Miracles: Medical, Psychological and Religious Reflections

John Meyendorff

I believe that at this later hour it is somewhat difficult for us to speak of deep spiritual matters and miracles, but I am emboldened by the fact that the Lord performed his first miracle at the wedding feast where people were drinking wine and having a good time. It is important to believe that God is with us in whatever we are doing. I will point to two or three major presuppositions about what we, being Christians, call miracles.

The first major presupposition that I think is essential for us to realize is that the world in which we live, the life that is ours, our experience of the spiritual and physical reality around us—something that we know very well—is not exactly what God intended His world to be. This presupposition is basic to the entire Christian faith: The world was created at the beginning, but some kind of derailment contrary to God's will occurred almost immediately. Something, somewhere, in creation—something in which we are involved very directly, existentially, and deeply—is wrong. The will of God is being betrayed. If one takes the world as it is around us as normal, as the one that God created, one realizes that one has to allow for God's creating evil, creating suffering, creating death, creating agony and all the terrible tragedy that surrounds us every day. But we know that God does not create evil. God is *not* responsible for evil. Evil, therefore, is a kind of external element in the reality of the cosmos, an element that God does not want.

I will not go into further explanations of the reasons for this situation. All

121

philosophers and all theologians have tried to explain the origins of evil, but no one has succeeded. Nevertheless, it remains as one of the most real facts of our life. Many people actually lose their faith because of that reason: "If God wants the world to be the way it is, I don't want that God." Many people reason that way, and of course they have a point. Now if one takes the Tradition, the thinking, the thoughts of the fathers, he or she discovers specific pointers that explain the condition of the world as it is and what is wrong with it. Both the New Testament and the Tradition of the Church speak of death as being the major—the last—enemy. The Book of Revelation of St. John says that the "last enemy" will be destroyed. Death is what he is talking about: the last—the ultimate—enemy.

In Scripture and in Christian thought, death is indeed physical death, but it is also something greater than that. There is also a spiritual death and a spiritual mortality that is even more real than physical death. Both are somehow connected. Death is something that God did not want but that is nevertheless a central reality in the life of the world and in our experience. Furthermore, we can say at this point that death has a moral dimension: It is related to sinfulness. This connection can be described in a variety of ways. This paper is not the place for a complicated theological lecture, but only an occasion to point at something central in the Greek patristic tradition. Death is seen by the Fathers of the Church as a central factor of our existence that makes sin inevitable. The Fathers are much more sophisticated than we might think; they do not simply believe that death is a punishment for sin—that we all die because we are bad people, as if God were pushing the button or pulling out the switch.

No! Death is a cosmic reality that is almost personalized—an objective reality in the world that also creates sinfulness. How does it create sinfulness? It makes death inevitable because it transforms the entire reality of the world into a desperate struggle for survival.

Darwin had a point when he described the world precisely in such a way. Are we not all struggling for survival all the time? The author of the Epistle to the Hebrews speaks in Chapter 3 of the fear of death as something that is the origin of sin. Sometimes I use this example with students: Picture two people together in a raft who have been shipwrecked. They have one pitcher of water and one piece of bread, and it will take them three weeks until they reach the shore. If they divide the water and the bread, they have no chance of survival; they will both die. But if one of them eats the bread and drinks the pitcher of water, he has a chance. So what happens? They have a fight. The stronger survives and gets to the shore.

This parable explains the relationship between nations, as well as between individuals. It can also explain the fact of our constant search for security. We all, for example, need to have a bank account. I have a monthly check because I have a job. Now that gives me relative comfort, but what anxiety, what anguish if it does not come; my security, my life and that of my family depend on it! But is it "ultimate security"? Millions of people are hungry. The fact that I just had a good meal and I have some security for tomorrow and for my family only delays the day when I will experience the universal power of death.

So, the temporary, illusory security given to me by my monthly check, by my insurance policy, and by my savings does in no way solve the ultimate problem of life and death, but it inevitably creates injustice—and therefore sin. I survive temporarily but at the expense of others. This statement is the reason that St. John Chrysostom once wrote that property creates injustice.

Now this idea does not square well with capitalistic ethics, but it is the rule by which our world exists. There is some injustice in the very fact that I have that illusory security. But why do I pretend that I have the right to have this meal? Because otherwise I am going to die. My health will deteriorate, so in addition I have a pension plan because I am so concerned about security in the future.

But this security is always, always at the expense of others. There is injustice in my struggle against death. I know that it is a very temporary struggle and that ultimately it just prolongs my life and does not solve the real problem. Now, we are coming to the topic: Which event *does* solve the problem in terms of what we believe?

The only event that does in fact solve this problem is the resurrection of Christ. That is why the resurrection is the "good news." The apostles said, "Good news! Death is no more; death has been conquered by death. There is hope." These two people on the raft could have safely shared this bread and water. They may have both drowned, but if they believed in God and in Christ, they would have had eternal life. It is because they fought against each other—not because they lacked food—that their death became the ultimate death. They only true miracle that really matters is the miracle of Christ's overcoming death. It is a miracle in the sense that it is an intervention of God in this fallen world and a sign of His power, which can be shared. It is really, authentically the only true miracle. All the other events that we call miracles are only signs and point to this one miracle.

Even the miracles performed by Christ in the gospels were temporary events. Lazarus rose from the dead, but he died again. The people who were healed from some disease—the epileptics—fell sick again. One of the most fascinating things in the New Testament is that you cannot be a Christian and believe in God and not believe in miracles, but all the miracles—other than the Resurrection of Jesus Christ—have only a relative significance. During the Middle Ages, people attributed miraculous qualities to all sorts of healings of this temporary nature, but now scientists and doctors are discovering that these healings can take place using drugs or surgery. They were miracles but so are the feats performed by medical science. Even so, both feats are ones of temporary relief.

It is obvious that, in the history of humanity, many more people have been actually healed by drugs and doctors than by miracle workers. Miracle workers perform some miracles from time to time to strengthen our faith, but millions and millions of other miracles are performed by people who just try to help their fellow beings. It is actually a secondary matter whether these healings come from science or from extraordinary means—by special divine intervention. All these miracles aim at one goal: To improve the quality of human life, to show concern for human suffering, and to try to alleviate it. This solidarity between people is something that in itself can be seen as a sign of the victory of the kingdom of God that is to come. But the ultimate final miracle is only that which was performed by Christ. St. Paul says that if Christ is not risen from the dead, our faith is in vain. Christ's resurrection was a real intervention of God in the reality of that life that gives content to our faith.

Now the last point I would like to make is the following: If we really believe that the world as it is now is *not* the world that God wanted it to be—that it is a corrupt, fallen world—then miracles and healings can be thought of as partial restorations of how God wants the world to be.

God certainly wants this world to be good. He created heaven and earth and said that "It is good." But then, afterwards, the world collapsed—not by His fault, but through an intrusion of other factors. All the miracles performed by Christ were actual but partial restorations of the original order of creation. The world is created according to the will of God, and God acts to fulfill that plan, not to modify it all the time. This argument is the theological argument and background for genetic engineering. To restore God's plan is fine, but to improve on what God did is questionable. The problem is to know the difference between God's will and man's ambition and presumption.

Those who practice medicine are in fact doing the same thing that our Lord Jesus Christ did—except, of course, that they are not God—and they see that their means limited. But their goal is the same. It is in His name, in cooperation with Him, by participation in His love for fellow creatures that they do what they do. Actually, the difference between what is a miracle and what is a successful medical operation is perhaps a little abstract. Perhaps we should not even be too concerned about it. But people are looking for miracles. They are sometimes superstitious, and we have to be tolerant about that. But the Lord Jesus Christ was not very tolerant of those people who looked for miracles for miracles' sake. "Miracles," He said, "will not be given to them except the miracles of Jonah the prophet"—that is, the miracle of the resurrection, which is the only miracle that is given free—the ultimate miracle.

In practice, what is important to discover is that the human concern for healing is also a concern of God's. God created the world, and He is the one who wants to restore it to goodness. He did the ultimate miracle and sacrifice by becoming a man, by rising from the dead, by conquering death. But we live in a period of human history where we still have the human freedom to do the right thing. We are called upon to cooperate with Him, to try to heal, and to share in His concern for the healing of man—both his soul and his body—with our limited means which continually increase with the progress of science. Another reason that this is part of the will of God is that man was made in the image of God. Man has been given the possibility to participate and to share in the healing and creative power of God, but only within the limits of God's will. If we want to be better than God, if we want to improve on what He has done, the real danger comes in. Moreover, it is in this desire to be as great or greater than God that the really demonic power appears. It is Satan who wants to be like God—and, in fact, to be better than God. He cultivates such aspirations among us as well. He tells us that if we want to, we can eat from one tree and not from the other so that we might create a superman on our own. This temptation is really the demonic temptation.

It is my duty as a theologian to point it out, to define it, and to talk about it. But those who are engaged in the responsible talk of scientific research and practice have the more difficult task of choosing the right options. Let us work together to acquire the same vision, the same intuition. This common work is our ultimate responsibility before God and humanity today.

of observation of measurement determines the outcome and gives reality to the particle or particles involved.

A particle does not even always behave like a particle. A fundamental tenet of quantum mechanics states that a particle exhibits both the properties of a particle and of a wave. Depending on our choice of experimental apparatus, we can observe an electron either as a localized particle or as wave spread out over a large area. However, under no circumstances can we ever observe an electron as both particle and wave at the same time.

Some physicists even prefer not to use the term *particle*. Instead, they speak of *elementary quantum phenomena*. For, indeed, how can the term *particle* be used to describe such strange entities? Consider the following property: Once two particle have been near each other, they will continue to affect each other instantaneously no matter how widely apart they become separated nor how fast they are speeding away from each other. Space and time seem to pose no obstacle to their ability to communicate instantaneously. Einstein, when confronted by such an idea, declared that he could not believe in a physics that involved "spooky actions at a distance." Unfortunately for Einstein, such "spooky" effects have been actually demonstrated in physics laboratories.

Paradoxes such as these are the everyday fare of working physicists. No wonder that a crisis of sorts has developed within the physics community. Quantum mechanics has been the most successful scientific theory in history, leading to such major applications as lasers, transistors, computers, and nuclear reactors, yet it has completely upset the commonsense notions of reality. In the words of one physicist: "One of the best-kept secrets of science is that physicists have lost their grip on reality."[2] Another physicist, speaking at a recent conference, summarized the issue as follows: "What are you willing to swallow as the truth? Quantum mechanics is telling us something about the nature of causality and reality. Nobody understands it, but we can't just ignore it."[3] Some physicists do ignore it, preferring to go about their work without worrying too much about its philosophical and metaphysical implications.

Other physicists, however, take the plunge into speculation, often in highly problematic ways. Books like *The Tao of Physics* and *The Dancing Wu Li Masters* have purportedly shown fundamental connections between modern physics and various Eastern religions but at the price of doing tremendous violence to both physics and the Eastern religions. The cosmic dance of the goddess Shiva finds its scientific justification or parallel in the chaotic, but paradoxically symmetric, "dance" of subatomic particles. A chain of books has followed, claiming quantum proofs for such phenomena as telepathy, levitation, reincarnation, the collective unconscious, cosmic consciousness, and so forth. About half the titles in

---

[2]Nick Herbert, *Quantum Reality,* Garden City, Doubleday, 1985, p. 15.
[3]*Science Digest,* July, 1986, p. 11.

the Bantam New Age Book series deal with physics and quantum mysticism. An attractively packaged example of how quantum theory has been put to the service of the New Age movement can be found in the little book *Space—Time and Beyond* by Bob Toben and Fred Alan Wolf (in the Bantam series).

Practically anything can be "proven" these days by magically, and usually irresponsibly, invoking the concept of a quantum jump. Even the origin of the universe itself can be represented as a gigantic quantum jump—not an unreasonable idea in itself, but one that has led to some far-out speculations, especially in the hands of Nobel prize-winning physicist, John Archibald Wheeler. In his view, the universe is a "self-excited circuit." It begins small at the Big Bang, grows in size, and gives rise to life and, eventually, to observers. The observers then participate in giving tangible "reality" to events that occurred long before there was any life anywhere. In Wheeler's view, the universe is no longer "out there" (as it is in Newtonian physics); we are personally involved in its evolution. The entirety of creation is built on billions upon billions of elementary acts of "oberver-participancy."

Wheeler's speculations are a particularly strong version of an idea that has a good following among physicists—namely, the Anthropic Principle. In its week, uncontroversial forms, the Anthropic Principle merely states that the observed properties of the universe are consistent with the existence of human life. If certain fundamental properties were even slightly different, life as we know it would never have arisen. But in its strong versions, the Anthropic Principle leads to a man-centered cosmology beyond the wildest dreams of pre-Copernican astronomy and theology. All of a sudden, man is not only back in the center of the universe but is the purpose for the existence of the universe. And we, as observers, in our turn bring the universe into existence. The result of such speculation can only be muddled metaphysics and mysticism.

The truth of the matter is that, contrary to popular belief, the conceit of science in this century has increased, rather than decreased. And yet, despite the various misguided attempts to create out of quantum theory all-encompassing explanations for everything, including life, consciousness, and the universe itself, the new universe that physics has revealed to us is a tremendously exciting place in which to live and think. It is an open, dynamic universe of interconnections and interpenetrations from the sub-microscopic scale of elementary particles to the behavior of cosmic space-time itself. There is unity in this universe, but a unity that is not static and predictable. There might even be some sort of teleological design built into the very fabric of this universe.

There is no need for Christian theology to wholeheartedly embrace the New Physics, and we certainly must not seek to accommodate our faith to current scientific theories. But we can engage in dialogue with this New Physics, and such dialogue might even give us new confidence in approaching the Gospel narratives and the ancient Tradition of the Church with an open mind—unprejudiced by the discredited assumptions of Bultmann and the various liberal theologies.

So, finally, we come to the question: What *is* the original Christian tradition concerning miracles, and how did it survive through the centuries? If we examine the accounts in the Gospels, we find that one common theme that runs through most of the miracles of Jesus is the theme of conflict. Jesus refers to his own miracles as "works," and they are works intended to recapture nature from the hostile powers of evil, sickness, and fragmentation. In the miracles of Jesus, God restores order and wholeness to his creation. In healing, Jesus deals with the whole person. He forgives people's sins and heals their souls, but He also heals their bodies. Suffering is intolerable to a loving God; suffering was not a part of the original plan for creation, so in the new creation it must be combatted. It is often stated that the major purpose of Jesus's miracles was to prove His divinity, but that is only part of the story: "Jesus did not heal people to prove that the was God; He healed them *because He was God.*"[4]

There is abundant evidence that miracles and healings took place in the Church throughout the first three centuries. There are reliable stories of miraculous healings in the writings of the Fathers, there are prayers for healing, and there is early evidence for the sacramental use of oil—what we call *euchelaion*, Holy Unction. The Church stood firm in its understanding of salvation as the redemption of the whole person against the Platonic/Manichaean view of the liberation of the soul from the body. In one of his most famous phrases, St. Irenaeus expressed the faith of the early Church: "The glory of God is a person fully alive."

However, this firmness of the Church lasted only until the era of Constantine. Dualistic ideas entered the Church in disguised, toned-down versions through the growing influence of the monks. In the ascetic practices of the Desert Fathers, mortification of the flesh became a prime objective. At the same time, among an increasingly secular clergy and leadership, the ability and, perhaps, even the desire to be channels for God's healing diminished. The ministry of healing went into a long eclipse, but the people's need for healing did not diminish.

At the same time, the very conception of God underwent major changes. In the East, with an increased emphasis on dogma, Jesus Christ became less and less God's mediator for man and increasingly the Almighty, stern Judge. He became more and more unknowable and unreachable. People felt unworthy to come before Him. In the West, even more drastic changes were underway. With the barbarian invasions and the collapse of civilization, God was more easily comprehended as a God of wrath than a God of love. This concept coupled with Augustinian theology and the ascetic influence, led to the notion of redemptive suffering. Sickness is sent by God as a punishment or penance to lead man to repentance. To pray for healing was tantamount to opposing God's will. The ministry of healing almost disappeared in the Western Church, and the Sacrament of Unction was transferred into a

---

[4]Francis MacNutt, *Healing,* Notre Dame, Ave Maria Press, 1974, p. 108.

Sacrament of last rites—Extreme Unction—to be administered at the point of death.

So in both East and West, radical changes occurred. In the East, God became distant and abstract, protected from both heretics and simple believers by a thick shield of dogmatic definitions. In the West, God became almost a pagan God, a sadistic Father. And on top of all this, the theology and leadership of the Church became decreasingly receptive to the idea of healing. Is it any wonder that in both parts of the universal Church people fled to the compassion of Mary and the saints? Relics and, later, icons became instruments of God's healing. Of course, with this increasingly popular devotion to the saints, a superstitious and magical understanding of miracles increasingly took hold. The saints came to be treated almost as pagan demi-gods, while the veneration of relics and icons has often transgressed the bounds of the appropriate and the theologically defensible.

The time has come for the Church to seek to recover the ancient ministry of healing. God's grace works through all possible means, including relics and icons, but I believe that He wills for us to be bonded as a community where compassion and prayer will once again become the primary channels of healing. To pray for healing in the name of Jesus is not to invoke a magical formula but to see people as Jesus would see them and to call on His strength to do what He Himself did when He walked the face of the earth. The ministry of healing is not an optional luxury. It is central to the Gospel and to the message of salvation. It means taking the Incarnation and the Resurrection seriously as living realities, not merely as historical doctrines. Above all, it is an act of obedience. God wants His Church to be a healing community, where his power is manifest. The tragic split that persists in the Church—between theologians and clergy, on the one hand, who often take an almost apologetic stance toward miracles, and the mass of believers, on the other had, who deeply yearn for healing—must finally be brought to an end.

This paper has attempted to do two things: First, to give a sample of the new scientific climate and the universe that is unfolding to our understanding—a universe very different from the exclusive universe of Newton and the liberal theologians who sought to do away with the very idea of miracles; second, by pointing out some of the distortions within the Church's own life and theology, to suggest a return to a more integral, holistic view of human needs.

Christians need not be embarrassed by miracles. Instead of seeing miracles as God overturning or interfering with the course of nature, we can more positively see them as ordering events—restoring and creating order and wholeness where it is lacking or has been damaged. This concept is the original Christian understanding of miracles, a view that is not inconsistent with the current climate in physical science. Miracles tell us something about the movement and direction of creation: "These events confront one with the evidence that this is God's world, after all—a dangerous and vital world of unlimited, living possibilities, in which no open-minded man can become bored. It is the kind of world for which man longs, but for which he had not dared to hope."[5]

In returning to my opening question, I offer this answer: Yes, it is possible to believe in miracles today as the early Christians did, but not only *as* the early Christians believed but beyond that belief to a belief in a revitalized theology that is in *creative dialogue* with modern science, especially physics. Such a combining of theological and scientific forces could lead us to see even more deeply, and with greater understanding, God's marvelous ways in nature. We have a personal and collective responsibility to pray earnestly that God's healing power will once again be manifest among us, who are called to be the living saints.

---

[5]Morton T. Kelsey, *Healing and Christianity*, New York, Harper and Row, 1973, p. 342.

Therapeutic Touch: Using Your Hands for Help or Heal

Karen Piligian

"Our hands are a gift. Through them we channel love in our hearts to suffering around us."
> —Richard Gordon

Therapeutic Touch is a method of facilitating healing that comes from the laying-on of hands. The technique used by the therapeutic touch is based on the assumptions that human beings have complex patterns of energy and that disease is associated with disorder, deficit, and/or blockage of the energy flow both within the individual and between the individual and the environment. Therapeutic touch is essentially a meditative process that is motivated by compassion and is focused by a clear intent to help another. It is viewed as a natural potential in human beings.

Body tissues are made up of molecules, which are made up of atoms, which are made up of protons, neutrons, and electrons, which produce energy. The activity in the neuro-muscular system occurs by means of electrical conductance. The electromagnetic field of a person, which is what is assessed during therapeutic touch, can be photographed by Kirlian photography. From photographs of people's magnetic fields, one can see that the intensity and color of the fields change with emotions.

Although the history of laying-on of hands goes back to early historical times, the scientific investigation of healing is very recent. In the early 1960s, Bernard Grad, a biochemist at McGill University, collaborated with R. V. Cadoret and G. I.

135

Paul at the University of Manitoba in an experiment to demonstrate that more than the "power of suggestion" was involved in the laying-on of hands. He obtained the cooperation of a renowned healer, Oskar Estebany of Montreal, and conducted double blind studies on mice and barley seeds.

In the first study, Grad selected 300 mice of the same size and weight and wounded them by cutting an oval of skin along their spine. They were randomly assigned to one of three treatment groups. The first group was allowed to heal without any outside intervention as a control. The second group received treatment by Estebany, who held the mice in his hands for fifteen minutes twice a day, five hours apart. The remainder were held by medical students who did not profess to heal.

To assess the effects of the treatment, a two-way analysis of variance was used. On the fifteenth and sixteenth day after wounding the mice, the mean surface area of the wounds in the group of mice treated by Estebany was significantly smaller than that of the other two groups.[1]

At a later date (1964, 1967), again using the services of Estebany, Grad developed another double blind study using barely seeds. Before the experiment, he soaked the seeds in a saline solution to simulate a "sick condition." He then divided the seeds in groups similar to the ones used in the experiment on mice. It was found that the seeds that were watered with fluid from flasks held by Estebany sprouted more quickly than the seeds in the control groups, that these sprouts grew taller, and that they contained more chlorophyll than the controls.[2]

In 1967, another biochemist who was also an enzymologist, Sr. Justa Smith, was motivated by Grad's studies to develop further research on the laying-on of hands. Her basic assumption was that should an energy change occur during healing, from whatever means, it should be apparent in the body's enzyme activity, for it is the enzymes that are crucial to the basal metabolism of the body. In her laboratory at Rosary Hill College, Buffalo, she developed a double blind study using the enzyme trypsin (1972) and Estebany as the healer. Dividing the trypsin into four flasks, she subjected one to high ultraviolet rays to break the bonding sites and thus simulate a "sick condition." This solution, as well as a second unaltered solution of trypsin, was held by Estebany for seventy-five minutes each day. The third sample was kept in its native state as a control, while the fourth sample was subjected to a high magnetic field (8,000-13,000 gauss). It was noted that the exposure of the trypsin solution to the laying-on of hands was qualitatively and quantitatively similar to that of the magnetic field when their daily relative percents of activity were

---

[1]Marianne D. Borelli and P. Heidt, eds., *Therapeutic Touch* Springer Publishing Co., New York, 1981, p. 4.

[2]Dolores Krieger, "Therapeutic Touch: The Imprimatur of Nursing," *AJN*, Vol. 75, 1975, p. 2.

graphed.[3] Smith repeated these test with other healers, three people who claimed to have healing abilities and three who did not. None of these subjects had an effect on the enzymes.

In 1971, the study was replicated with three other healers. Other enzymes were introduced into research: NAD (nicotinamide-adenine-dinucleotide) and amylase. When the healers treated the NAD, there was a decrease in activity.[4] None of the healers effected a change in the activity rate of amylase. Her conclusions were that the healer's ability does not affect all enzymes in the same way, and some are even unaffected.[5] However, the necessary effects all seem to contribute to improving or maintaining health.

Dolores Krieger—a Ph.D., an R.N., and a Professor of Nursing at New York University—was the first to study laying-on of hands in human subjects and from it developed a variation of the laying-on of hands called therapeutic touch.

In 1973, at the American Nurses' Association Ninth Conference of Nurse Researchers, Dr. Krieger reported her findings of a study she had conducted after she realized that a similarity exists between chlorophyll and hemoglobin. Krieger hypothesized that hemoglobin would be a sensitive indicator of energy change as well as of oxygen uptake and would be an appropriate test object in human subjects who were treated by the laying-on of hands. Krieger noted that the prophyrin structure of the hemoglobin molecule, which is responsible for oxygen uptake in the tissues, resembles the chlorine structure of chlorophyll in that both are derivative of the same biosynthetic pathways and that the nature and arrangement of their side chains are similar.[6] Whereas the chlorophyll molecule is patterned around an atom of magnesium, the porphyrin in hemoglobin is patterned around an atom of iron. Grad's earlier findings indicated an increase in chlorophyll in the barely sprouts treated by the laying-on of hands. Smith's research also indicated that some enzyme systems responded to laying-on of hands. The biosynthesis of hemoglobin is dependent upon numerous enzymatic transactions, among them ALA synthetase, ALA dehydratase, and ferriochelatase, and thus hemoglobin was chosen as the dependent variable for her experiments.

Krieger's hypothesis was the purposeful touching of an ill person, coupled with an intent to help or heal, will effect an elevation in the hemoglobin values of the ill person. Krieger used forty-six subjects in the experimental group and twenty-nine subjects in the control group. All subjects were controlled for the following variables: their pre-test Hgb values, their circadian cycles, whether they smoked tobacco, whether they had had recent trauma, if they had a history of a recent change in vital signs—all of which can significantly change Hgb levels.

---

[3]Borelli, p. 5.
[4]*Ibid.*, p. 6.
[5]*Ibid.*, p. 6.
[6]*Ibid.*

Pretest samples of blood were drawn on all subjects. Following the laying-on of hands, post-test samples of blood were drawn from subjects in both the experimental group and the control group. The results verified the hypothesis that the post-test Hgb values of the experimental group would be greater than the pre-test means at the 0.01 level of confidence.[7] There was no significant change in the post-test means of the control group.

In a second experiment (1974), Krieger used professional registered nurses as "healers." Patients who were to receive therapeutic touch were in the experimental group; those who were to receive routine nursing care without therapeutic touch were in the control group. In addition to the controls used in the initial research, Krieger controlled for meditational practices and breathing exercises by the subjects. The technicians analyzing the blood samples were not informed that research was in progress, and all the blood samples were analyzed by the same machine.

There were thirty-two patients and sixteen nurses in each group, each nurse working with two patients. Pre-test blood samples were drawn for both Hgb values and Hct (hematocrit) ratios on all patients. Therapeutic touch was then administered to the experimental group on two consecutive days by nurses taught to do this intervention by Krieger. Post-test samples were drawn a minimum of four hours after the last treatment by therapeutic touch. The data supported the hypothesis that the mean Hgb values of patients treated by therapeutic touch changed significantly following this treatment at a 0.01 level of confidence.[8]

In her doctoral dissertation, the first on therapeutic touch, P. Heidt, a registered nurse in private practice in New York City, used a standardized anxiety questionnaire for ninety patients admitted to a cardiovascular unit. An experimental group of thirty then received five minutes of therapeutic touch. The nurses did not promise healing or pain relief. A second group of thirty patients received casual touch—that is their pulse was taken in four places by a nurse who stayed in the room five minutes but didn't speak to them. A third control group of thirty was visited by a nurse who did not touch the patient but sat and talked to them for five minutes. The results were clear. When the patients filled out a second version of the anxiety questionnaire to measure how they felt after the nurse's visit, the therapeutic touch group showed a decrease in anxiety that was significant at a 0.01 confidence level.[9] The casual touch group showed a decrease in anxiety but not at a significant level. Some patients in the third group actually showed an increase in anxiety.

A characteristic pattern of therapeutic touch that occurs in a majority of patients includes the following:

---

[7]*Ibid.*, p. 7.

[8]*Ibid.*

[9]Ronni Sandroff, "A Skeptic's Guide to Therapeutic Touch," *RN*, January 1980, Vol. 43, No. 1, p. 27.

1)   The healee's voice level goes down several decibels.

2)   The healee's respiration slows down and deepens.

3)   The patient gives an audible sign of relaxation, a deep breath, or sigh or states, "I feel relaxed."

4)   An observable peripheral flush may be noted on the patient's face or on his or her whole body, which is due to the dilation of the peripheral vascular system during the healer/healee interaction.

Basic to therapeutic touch is the concept that a human being is a highly complex field, or continuum of various life energies. The physical body can be looked upon as the denser or more compacted aspect of the field. There is also a constant exchange between the individual and the environment.

When implementing therapeutic touch, healers sensitize their hands to the energy field and assess its condition. They then knowledgeably help the patient to repattern his or her energies in a healthier way. The process of therapeutic touch involves three essential steps. More than one step occurs at the same time; however, for the purposes of this explanation, they will be separated into three distinct steps:

1)   *One must be centered.* Consciously centering oneself puts one into a very calm, alert state of being. If one's thought are scattered or emotionally upset, the healing process is blocked. To be centered means to be focused totally on healing and being a channel for this universal energy flow—God, love, the Christ Light. If the healer projects an outcome and is anxious for the patient to get well, healing is not effective. After I am centered, which I sometimes do by imagining a white light coming through the top of my head and out through my hands and feet, I say, "Thy Will be done." The Jesus Prayer, "Lord, Jesus Christ, Son of God have mercy upon me a sinner" repeated several times can also help one center oneself; it can also be used in daily meditation.

2)   After becoming centered, one must find the differences in the body's magnetic field, which is called the *assessment.* Human beings are open systems, and the human field is bilaterally symmetrical. There is an input, through-put, and output of energy. Placing one's hands approximately six inches from the body, one slowly feels the field from the head to the feet. Depending on the patient, I feel either hot or cold spots or "congestion" in an area of imbalance.

3)   The third step in the process of therapeutic touch involves directing and modulating the energy. What does one do about the differences he or she feels in the person's field? There is no scientific basis for this. Researchers have not been able as yet to answer the how and why.

Important to the implementation of therapeutic touch is the healer's intention.

The healer must have a sincere intent to help another. He or she should also be in good health. When I have a cold, I cannot sense the field with my hands, and my energy flow is blocked. One must also come to terms with why he or she is playing the role of healer.

Because the energy field is a continuum, whatever one does to one aspect will have an effect on the whole. The concept of wholeness is crucial in implementing therapeutic touch. A nurse I used to work with at a clinic in Flushing, New York, asked me to "do my thing." She had a headache and a backache. After giving her therapeutic touch, she informed me her headache and backache were gone but now her ears were clogged! I then had to go back and brush out the discomfort, realizing that I had not been working with the field as a whole.

Children and adults are treated no differently when using the therapeutic touch. However, children and infants—as well the elderly—have very sensitive systems, and, as with medication, therapeutic touch must be administered in smaller and more gentle doses. Too much or an incorrect repatterning can cause discomfort.

In holistic medicine, the patient takes responsibility for his or her own health and illness rather than playing a passive role in recovering. When energy is given to a patient, it is the patient who decides how to use it. The secondary gains of illness might come into play. A patient might have less responsibility at work or at home or be paid more attention to when he or she is ill. Attitudes and emotions have a very definite effect on the well-being of a person and the course of an illness and need to be assessed.

Many who call me for therapeutic touch usually do it as a last resort. They have "tried everything." A student nurse assigned to one of my patients saw me doing therapeutic touch to relieve nausea and pain in a cancer patient. She then asked if I would see her father, who had recently started chemotherapy. I met Mr. M. and his family that weekend. My nursing assessment included a physical assessment, a medical and a family history, and a nutritional assessment, which included any medications he was taking. The psychological assessment included family interactions as well. We talked about whether he was at all religious and if he prayed. He had been brought up as a Catholic, but his mother was Greek Orthodox. He was familiar with imagery and visualization but did not use these techniques on a regular basis. He was a science teacher at a local high school and was very well liked and respected by staff and student. He was 51 years old and the father of three girls, the youngest of whom was sixteen years old. He had cancer of the colon, which had been removed a few months earlier. He had started on chemotherapy after the doctors had found that the cancer had spread to the liver. By the time of my visit, Mr. M. told me that the cancer had metastasized and the doctors had given him three months to live.

I explained the process of therapeutic touch but did not guarantee anything. He was willing to take the responsibility of working towards his own well-being. In the beginning, I visited him twice a week to do therapeutic touch. When I was there, we went through a relaxation exercise as well as using the white light. For fifteen minutes three times a day, Mr. M. would visualize the chemotherapy and his own immune system fighting off the cancer cells while being in the relaxed state. By the end of two weeks, some of the side effects from the chemotherapy had subsided. He was still losing some of his hair, but his appetite had returned. He was not as tired and weak as he had been, and his nausea was gone. By the end of six weeks, the tumor in his lung had shrunk 1/2 cm. in density. The lung was where the least improvement had been expected. Also, during his course of treatments, the pressure in his eyes had lowered. He had glaucoma, and the eye doctor found that his eyes had improved and subsequently decreased his medication. After five and a half months, his checkup at Sloan Kettering revealed only a shadow in his lung. His spleen was no longer enlarged, his colon was clear, and his liver was fine. He remained on chemotherapy. Sixteen months later, Mr. M. passed away. I visited him in the hospital a week before he died. He said, "I'm not afraid of dying; I just do not want to leave such a young family."

In the beginning, I came to Mr. M's help in any way I could with what knowledge I had. I was the one who felt like a student. I learned so much from Mr. M. that helped my own growth, but I also saw much growth in Mr. M. as the months passed. The quality of his life was better, and he was productive until the last month before he died. He was unlike other cancer patients in that he was not bedridden. He jogged at least three times a week, put in a skylight in the living room, and had so much spirit. He was at peace with himself, and his fear of dying disappeared. At his funeral, his sister was talking with me and said, "He had so much faith that you would help him, but nothing can beat cancer." His family had not grown as Mr. M. had. I realized myself that physical healing was not what was intended for him.

Rob was 37-year-old airline manager with two little children and another on the way. He was operated on to remove a tumor on his lung. Soon after that, he started on chemotherapy. After quite a few months, I was asked to see him. I again did physical, psychological, and nutritional assessments of him and asked about his beliefs. He was Catholic but never went to church and did not usually pray. He was having a lot of difficulty tolerating the chemotherapy. I went through a relaxation exercise with him, which he did for ten to fifteen minutes three times a day. I would also go twice a week to his home to give him therapeutic touch. By the second week, the side effects from the chemotherapy had improved. Rob had been on chemotherapy for one year. He now goes for checkups ever six months and has been free of cancer for three years. Prayer is very much part of his life, and one can see a calming change in him emotionally. Recently, I learned that when the surgeon had opened him up, he did not remove anything. Rob had tumors everywhere, and there was nothing the doctor could do. Rob did not know this and does not know it to this day. His wife did not want him to know. I think that if he had known how poor his prognosis was, he would not be here now to enjoy watching his new daughter growing up.

Toni was a woman in her thirties who was admitted to the hospital for acute asthma. It was a little after midnight, and Toni rang for the nurse in a panic. She could not breathe. She was not able to have bronchosol treatment because it had been administered only an hour before, so I asked if I could try some therapeutic touch. She was familiar with it and was willing to try it. After I centered myself, I placed my hands on her shoulders and almost immediately she calmed down. Her respiration slowed and deepened, and she began shouting how marvelous this was! She was then able to fall back to sleep.

Ellen, a friend and a nurse with whom I work, came to me one day and asked, "I know I always laugh at you and I think this is nonsense, but would you do your touch on my leg." Ellen had had a pain in her calf for about a week, and it was getting worse. She had tried everything and was going to go to the doctor if it did not get better soon. I worked on her for about five minutes and asked her how she felt. She was not sure. She still felt pain. I said I had tried, and we left it at that. The next day she came over to me to say that her pain was gone. After she had gotten home, she realized that the pain was no longer there.

Another patient, Mrs. P., who had just had a shunt put into her arm for dialysis, was taking pain medication every four hours. She complained of being in pain, but it was too soon for medication. I asked if she would like me to try therapeutic touch. I did, but nothing happened. The next day Mrs. P. came to me and said that her arm had become much better about an hour after the treatment. She did not need any pain medication until bedtime and slept well that night.

Therapeutic touch is an extension of a nursing skill. Perhaps it is because touch is so primitive a need that it is so powerful as a fundamental therapeutic tool. One can hardly imagine the basic nursing skills being performed without the act of touch. An infant can live being blind, deaf, and without the sense of smell and taste. However, without touch an infant can waste away and die.

Therapeutic touch involves an undefinable but learnable method of balancing human energy. The caring and love that are involved and doing this balancing makes us aware that each of us is connected in some way and that we do give of ourselves to each person who crosses our paths.

Notes on Contributors

John Breck, Ph.D., is professor of New Testament and Ethics at St. Vladimir's School of Theology, Crestwood, New York.

John T. Chirban, Ph.D., Th.D., is professor of psychology and co-director of the Office of Counseling and Spiritual Development at Hellenic College and Holy Cross School of Theology, and serves as an affiliate in human development at Harvard University, Cambridge, Massachusetts.

Demetrios J. Constantelos, Ph.D., is Charles Cooper Townsend distinguished professor of history and religious studies at Stockton State College, Stockton, New Jersey.

John Demakis, M.D., is professor of medicine at the Stritch School of Medicine, Loyola University, Maywood, Illinois.

Peter H. Diamandis, M.D., is president and chairman of the Board of International Space University, Cambridge, Massachusetts.

Milton Efthimiou, Ph.D., is director of the Office of Church and Society, Greek Orthodox Archdiocese, New York, New York.

Nicholas D. Kokonis, Ph.D., is a clinical psychologist, Chicago, Illinois.

Nicholas J. Krommydas, is instructor in pastoral theology and co-director of the Office of Counseling and Spiritual Development, Hellenic College and Holy Cross School of Theology, Brookline, Massachusetts.

John Meyendorff, Ph.D., is professor of church history and Dean of St. Vladimir's School of Theology, Crestwood, New York.

Bishop Nicholas is Primate of the Carpatho-Russian and Orthodox Church.

George J. Pazin, M.D., is associate professor of medicine at the University of Pittsburgh School of Medicine, Pittsburgh, Pennsylvania.

Peter Poulos is director of training in the department of Pastoral Care at the Methodist Hospital, Brooklyn, New York.

Georgia Photopulos is patient care consultant to the National Cancer Institute, National Institute of Health, Bethesda, Maryland.

Karen Piligian, R.N., is a dietician and nurse, Brooklyn, New York.

Constantine Sarantidis is assistant pastor of St. Andrew's Greek Orthodox Church, Chicago, Illinois.

Theoharis C. Theoharides, Ph.D., M.D., is associate professor of biochemistry, pharmacology, and psychiatry and serves as director of medical pharmacology at Tufts University School of Medicine.

About the Editor

JOHN T. CHIRBAN, Ph.D., Th.D., is Professor of Psychology and Co-Director of Counseling and Spirituality Development at Hellenic College and Holy Cross School of Theology, Brookline, Massachusetts. He is an Affiliate in Human Development at Harvard University, and Director of Cambridge Counseling Associates in Cambridge, Massachusetts.

Among Dr. Chirban's recent writings are *The Interactive-Relational Approach to Interviewing: Encountering Lucille Ball and B. F. Skinner* (University Press of America, 1991); *Healing: Interdisciplinary Perspectives in Medicine, Psychology, and Religion* (Editor and contributor, Holy Cross Press, 1991); "Developmental Stages in Eastern Orthodoxy," *Transformations of Consciousness* (Kenneth Wilbur, Random House, 1986); *Coping with Death and Dying—An Interdisciplinary Approach* (Editor and contributor, University Press of America, 1985); and *Youth and Sexuality* (Hellenic College Press, 1985).